MAN BEING

Volume II: *Go to the Light*

MAN BEING

Volume II: *Go to the Light*

Communicated to
Dramos & Bohemias

Copyright © 2019 by Dramos & Bohemias

All rights reserved. This book may not be reproduced in whole or in part, or transmitted in any form, without permission from the authors, except by a reviewer who may quote brief passages in a review; nor may any part of this book be reproduced, stored in a retrieval system or transmitted in any form or by any means electronic, mechanical, photocopying, recording, or other, without written permission from the authors.

Front cover design by James Lee Chiahan

ISBN 978-1-9991777-2-0

This is not a philosophical dialogue. You are being asked to use the tools that have always been available to Man Being. This book is redefining your understanding about time and redefining your understanding about travel. Time travel is awaiting you and this is simply an exercise in once again reconnecting these two beliefs – time and travel. Reconnect and reabsorb.

TABLE OF CONTENTS

Prologue

Introduction

Chapter 1 – The Preparation   1
Females Show the Way, Launching from 5D, Unanswered Questions
Your Family is Growing, Making Room for the Universe
A New History

Chapter 2 – Shape Shifting   11
Wolf & Dog Mythology, Neuri Tribe of Shifters
The Capitoline Wolf, The Shepherd Tale, Werewolf Folklore
The Etruscan Minotaur

Chapter 3 – Mithras   29
The Mithraeum, Imitation Cults, Origin of the Judicial System
Women had the Knowledge, Animal Sacrifice, Our Planet is a Prison
Constellations are Beliefs

Chapter 4 – The Channel   46
Afterlife Instructions, Loved Ones in Lyra, The Afterlife Proposition
Meeting the Source, The Truth about Medusa, Revisit the Aten

Chapter 5 – The Nimbus   63
Not a Holy Hat, Designator for Sirius Beings
Clouded Information, Nimbus is The Channel, We are all Saints

Chapter 6 – The Garden of Eden   70
Return to the Tree, Not a Paradise, Eat the Apple
The Real Fall, The Bible is a Call for Help, The Sirius SOS

Chapter 7 – Michelangelo's Lost Statue — 81
Coded Fountain, Ancient Symbols, Michelangelo's Priapus
Fertility & Ouroboros, The Secret Sect of Christianity
True Baptism, The Bulls of San Nicola di Bari

Chapter 8 – Procreation — 98
What is Reproduction, Caligula Destroyed the Light, Ghost Energy
Procreation is not Repair, Splitting our Energy, What is the Orgasm

Chapter 9 – Music — 111
Hip Hop as a Tool, Acid Jazz and EDM, A World Without Music
The Key of D, Jazz and Time Travel, Listen to 'Round Midnight
Frank Sinatra's My Way, The Rat Pack

Chapter 10 – The Tower — 137
Lady Liberty or Chimera, Seattle Space Needle, Amusement Parks
Eiffel Disconnect, Tower of Babel, Sirius Beings in America
9/11 Attacks, The High-Rise

Chapter 11 – Orion DRA — 157
Enslavement Program, Clipped Wings, Mining Gold
Feeding off of our Ascension, DRA Origin Story, Area 51 Agenda
The Truth about Climate Change, What is Lightning
Trapped in Form

Chapter 12 – Nikola Tesla — 178
We are Self-Generators, Discovering Time Travel
Multi-layered Existence, Second Body in Lyra, Tesla's Arrival
Dematerializing into Gaseous State

Chapter 13 – Déjà Vu — 192
Remembrance of the Light Body, Rename to Reconnection
No Past/Present/Future, The Spiral Movement, One-Sided Mirror
Déjà vu is like Swimming, The Primordial Sea

Chapter 14 – Fe|Male   203
No Gender in Light, Super Female Form, Sappho was a Lyra Being
Euripides' Secret, Dionysia Festival and Freemasonry
Cleopatra Saved the Texts, The Almost New World Order

Chapter 15 – The Altered State   219
Tripping on DMT, A Broken Apart Experience, Psychedelic Trap
Eating with God, Mother Nature Allegory, Our True Atmosphere
Millennials Unite

Chapter 16 – Persephone & Demeter   235
An Opening in Time, The Whirling Motion
The Underworld of Truth, Hades Saved Persephone
Don't Fear Cerberus, Waiting in Lyra, Demeter and the Fire
Return of the Divine Feminine

Chapter 17 – The Elysian Field   248
The Eleusis Ascension Event, Elysian Field State, Old Portal
Eleusinian Mysteries, Dramos & Bohemias Mission
Carlos Schwabe and the Elysian Fields, Attracting Other Beings

Chapter 18 – The Plant World   262
Another Dimension of Experience, Fluid Movement of Plants
State of Travel and Motion, Growing in all Directions
Lyra's Fertile Soil, The Hand of God, Root Origin
Kaleidoscope Experience, Return of Terra

Chapter 19 – Beyond Earth   273
The Hidden Earth, It's a Causeway, Massive Implosion
Plants are Beacons of Light, Inside out Experience
The True Force of Nature, The Sirius Connection

Chapter 20 – The Passageway   284
Contacted by The Dead, This is a Directory
Famous People Tell All, Opened up a Gateway
Readers Are No Longer Passive, Removed from 3D, The Rose

PROLOGUE

  This is an ongoing dialogue between Dramos, Bohemias and Beings from the Intermediary World of Lyra. Lyra is the World in which we reassemble our Light Body. It is the World of Light at the "end of the tunnel", which has been described in many near death experience accounts. We are all participants in this communication and your commitment is pivotal for the Soul Ascension Group Assembly. The following guidance was offered to us on June the 26th of 2019, at the onset of assembling Volume 2.

"You must read this book as you would experience a dream – with childlike abandon. Return to your imagination. That is where we are waiting for you all."

INTRODUCTION

This is an undertaking to reassemble the truth of our origin and to assist others in their understanding. Volumes 1 and 2 are therefore a preliminary understanding and not a final version of the understanding. Please remember that many of these ideas are foreign and will need to be assimilated and absorbed in stages. This is a primary introduction to a complex construct and restructuring of belief. It is profoundly shifting the group consciousness of Beings who are involved in the mission to return homeward.

We are assembling the dissemination so that the absorption will continue in stages and the belief can be reconstructed. Our origin story has been maligned, reconstructed and grossly misinterpreted to derail our entire existence. The dissemination of the Man Being book series is a responsibility to reintroduce the truth. This is not something that can be introduced in one chapter or one book. It is a monumental undertaking and will include several Volumes.

Volume 2 introduces the understanding and belief of the Source of our Light. This is a central idea and a centralized belief. It is a revelation and remembrance that will allow us to go forth and not only reclaim the origin story, but redefine how we will get there. **You are encouraged to share the information, as you are also participating in the dissemination of this material.**

1

The Preparation

There is more emphasis on female energy in Volume 2. Why is it important for female readers to absorb the information in these books?

> There is an initiative to bring more light into your existence. What you are referring to as "female" is in fact a closer experience with light. The female energy is a closer experience to a more holistic absorption of what light is all about. You are introducing readers to "female figures" or archetypes, as women are in fact closer recipients of light. The female energy is playing a significant role in the ascension journey homeward – to the light integration and consciousness.

Women are essential to the success of the Repair Project. Is that what you're saying?

> Yes, although we will be correcting your understanding of the "gender divide". **Those Beings who are identifying as females are closer to the holistic integration and reconnection of light consciousness.** You are reintegrating components of light that you have lost a connection with. The female energy is mostly what you are lacking. Beings that are identifying as "gender-neutral" are still biased in the female energy, as this is a massive component of light consciousness and absorption.

How will readers be affected by reading Volume 2?

> They will – undoubtedly – no longer be interested in male and female roles. There is a movement away from these designations and there will be a sense that your readers no longer wish to be involved in the current gender paradigm or split.

Will the designation of "family" also change by consequence?

> Your idea of "family" will expand. We are suggesting that you are re-believing what a family unit involves. As your ascension journey unfolds, you will reconnect with other Light Beings who are part of your Soul Ascension Group and therefore light reassembly experience.

What is the main revelation contained in Volume 2?

> You will be reminded of the enjoyment of light and will be reconnecting with your Source. You have been cut off from your Source and the reconnection is not simply an emotional experience – it is your lifeblood. You are correcting the lack of light. The deprivation is being shifted so that there is now light flowing toward you and flowing out from you. There is a circuit that is operating again. You are learning how to generate your light. This is the entire point of Volume 2, as this Volume is the preparation.

What exactly is Volume 2 a "preparation" for?

> We are preparing you for the release of your light.

This dialogue is proposing a seismic shift in belief and is bound to leave the Reader with a myriad of questions. Will this hamper their reconnection?

> Unanswered questions are equivalent to forming a space to allow further beliefs to be contained in. Questions are an excellent way to further the momentum of the ascension energy, for if one does not have any questions then there is no further room to reintegrate new beliefs. There must be questions in order for the experience of ascension to continue. If there are no questions then you have completed your ascension journey and the dialogue is no longer necessary.

Will the table of contents or book summary deter readers?

> Reading a table of contents or summary as opposed to experiencing the words and therefore the belief, are two separate propositions. Those who wish to read summaries and dismiss the information are clearly not interested in pursuing a new level of belief. Those Beings who are interested in the homeward journey and are part of the Sirius experience will undoubtedly be focused and interested in opening up the chapters and communicating the material to others.

Volume 2 examines more historical inaccuracies while introducing new concepts and beliefs. Will this turn off readers who aren't interested in history?

> Those readers who are not "interested" in reading about history are not necessarily bored by it. They are – on an unconscious level – rejecting its

inaccuracies and therefore relevancy to their existence. This is in fact the very reason that they will want to read Volumes 1 and 2. By pointing out this fact these readers will make room for a new approach to history. These readers will learn a new history that they feel applies to them and is in fact in alignment with their own beliefs. By absorbing these new beliefs you will expand your pattern of consciousness and continue your journey of ascension.

That may be true, but some readers just want to know what God is and how the universe was created. They don't want the "stuff in between". Why can't we just address the grand questions and ascend?

We are asking for you to plan for awareness by reassembling your beliefs in awareness. The preparation is allowing you to experience an enormous paradigm change. Some of your readers may claim that they are prepared for the knowledge about "God and the Creation". The truth is that you do not have the space for such a massive reintegration, as you have not yet removed so many of your current beliefs. You must make room for new beliefs. The shift in belief that is required to answer the God/universe question is a great one, which requires an enormous level of commitment to redefine what you believe and what you no longer believe. The discarding of belief requires preparation. You are asking about accepting a new belief when there is no room, as you have not already discarded outdated beliefs.

Will Volume 2 offer a similar high or experience to Volume 1?

>Volume 2 is an exceptional experience in this book series. There is an emphasis on preparing and continuing to expand your awareness to allow room for the monumental shift in belief that is presented in Volume 3. We must correct with you the historical and cultural misunderstandings that are highlighted in Volume 2. The elimination of these previously regarded truths will create space for the newfound and reconnected beliefs that you will absorb in Volume 3. This is a Volume upon which you are shifting and reprioritizing not only your beliefs about the 3rd density, but you are preparing a strong connection with the 5D experience.

What is the 5D experience and why are we skipping over 4D?

>We are of course speaking of the 5th density when we use the term 5D. Density is the availability of the light and the speed of light that you are able to absorb. Your Earth plane density is 3D and is defined by form and containment of light – a prison state. The 4D or 4th density experience is the adjustment from 3rd density and the release toward the 5th density. The 5D experience is the launching frequency for time travel.

Are we guiding readers beyond Earth by the end of Volume 2?

>Yes. The Earth bound existence is what is being shifted in Volume 2. You are letting go of the understanding that the Earth is the only horizon of your belief. Understanding your origin not only

redefines the beginning but also awakens you to the reality that your Earth plane existence is in the dark.

Some readers might be thinking that we are writing science fiction. Will those readers still benefit from the experience?

> There is still somewhat of a suspicion about whether or not the work is a fiction. You must allow your readers to regard this as a fiction – if this is how they need to process the knowledge. They are absorbing the information whether or not it is presented as truth. Please understand that this is how the arts play an important role in dissemination, as art is a soft way to introduce complicated information. If they are following the work then they are absorbing it. Even if readers are entertained by the material and feel this is strictly fantasy, they are still absorbing. Absorbing is a requirement for your readers to continue the work.

How can someone absorb the information if they don't believe it to be true?

> If they are moving forward in the writings and interested in subsequent Volumes then they have formed a belief. The reconnection period is instantaneous when it occurs – but it does not always occur the moment somebody reads the words on the page.

Do readers have to see or speak with Lyra the way we are doing – to make the full reconnection?

> Dramos and Bohemias are functioning as interpreters. If you are reading the material or

hearing about the material or receiving the signal through someone else engaging in the material, you are making a connection. You have been taught that an extreme experience like the psychedelic "drug trip" is the benchmark. This is incorrect. Quietly shifting your beliefs does not have to be a tipping point or a decimation or an implosion. Many of you are seeking an "extreme experience" so that you can feel like you are reconnecting. This is not necessary.

You've previously mentioned that readers will be experiencing dreams or visions while absorbing the material. Is that how they will be "quietly shifting" their beliefs?

Yes. You are encountering a lot of your new experiences in dream state. Dreams are not always recalled upon your waking state. Many of you are experiencing the connections that we are speaking about in this state of awareness. Most of your reconnections are made during your sleeping state. Please trust that this is developing. You may experience an increase in fatigue for example, as you wish to sleep "more hours" and experience more reconnections.

To clarify, whether we recall our dreams or not, we are making reconnections in the sleeping state. Is that correct?

This is correct. You must trust and continue with the work. The connection with Lyra is not as extreme as you are imagining. You are encountering many of your experiences in the sleeping state, as this is the way for many of you to experience the reconnective patterns.

Should readers be absorbing the Volumes in chronological order?

> There is ultimately no requirement to read one Volume before another if one has already made their reconnections. What must be remedied is the need to advise readers on how to absorb the information. Your readers may discover that reading the chapters back to front and out of order may also provide an additional level of absorption and assistance in shifting belief. There is no necessary requirement to proceed in a linear capacity, as in reading chapters and Volumes in chronological order. You must allow your readers the freedom to read the Volumes as they choose.

What more can we offer the Reader as preparation for Volume 2?

> Your readers will benefit from knowing that the Man Being book series is a continuation of writings that were last disseminated in the 16th century AD. There were two attempts in this time period to release the information but the books were burned.

Has anything survived from those 16th century works?

> The original manuscript drafts are stored in the Vatican Library although not attributed to the original authors, as the material was stolen. The theft was by order of King Henry II, of France. This Being had a great interest in secret mystery schools and knowledge about alchemy and ascension.

Who were the original authors of the 16th century works?

You will be addressing the authorship in another Volume, as the information will be part of a larger reveal. There are key individuals in this linear time period who made massive contributions in writing and with their ideas. This was not a passive historical time period where books were simply absconded. This was a minefield in that there was a monumental and violent release of energy and containment of energy. There was a fight to prevent those who wished to ascend and therefore further contribute to the Repair Project.

2

Shape Shifting

Some readers of Volume 1 have reported feeling an awakening but also a distinct restlessness.

> When you wish to see yourself as the divine Ruler of your own source, then you will understand that the reason for the unrest is that you recognize a belief about yourself and a belief about your abilities.

Is the unrest also rooted in skepticism or a resistance to new beliefs?

> There are many levels of belief that your readers are reconnecting with. You will have a challenge in attempting to change the belief while also expressing how to change the belief. The understanding that you must believe while also changing your belief is the challenge that awaits you all.

Are you saying that confusion is inevitable while we reconnect with this information?

> Please accept that your readers must feel confused. Confusion is indicating a realignment and a reconnection. Confusion is equal to ascension in the early stages. It is a necessary feeling and experience that allows you to let go of beliefs while not immediately rushing to contain new and incorrect beliefs.

Confusion is indicating that we're making room for new beliefs.

> The confusion is allowing you the space to abandon old beliefs. This is the space that you must experience and be comfortable with. Confusion

opens the door to the space that you are occupying when you release the light.

You're describing confusion as empty space. Is this "space" akin to nothingness?

> You must master the experience of nothingness. The belief in nothingness and feeling comfortable in the nothingness will allow you to reconnect with the light and your true existence.

Are you asking readers to "suspend their disbelief" in order to believe?

> We are asking your readers to disbelieve their outdated beliefs. You are redefining the term "disbelief" in Volume 2, for "disbelieving" will now apply to the necessary release of your incorrect beliefs.

In other words, "suspend our outdated beliefs".

> Yes. More appropriately, devour them. This process is better understood as "reconnecting". You are reconnecting and reassembling what you already know.

What do you mean by "devour" the outdated beliefs?

> We will explain the precise use of this term through our next topic of discussion.

What is the topic?

MAN BEING

We would like to begin your Volume 2 with a discussion on shape shifting – or forming and reforming.

Is shape shifting part of the disconnect experience?

Yes. You are reforming as you shift your beliefs. The disconnect choice is a decision to shift your shape. You are learning that your form as Man Being is restrictive.

Is this an experience that others around us will witness?

It has been witnessed and these occurrences have been accounted for in your histories and mythologies.

What are the specific accounts?

This density of experience is one that is articulated through your wolf and dog mythology. These are the mythologies that bind all of you together, despite the difference in your ancestral origins to date. This is similar to the concept of water being contained in all of your physical form.

Are you suggesting that we are transitioning into a Wolf Being or that we contain wolf-like ability?

Shape shifting is the re-designation of energy and light in form. The mastery of shape shifting is experienced in a way that a form is created that has the resemblance of a wolf.

The form we shift into resembles a wolf and so we've interpreted it as a Wolf-Man, or as a Werewolf. Is that an accurate understanding?

> Yes. The Being you refer to as Herodotus has documented such cases, albeit naïvely. There was a conscious awareness and there was an ability of some to master this understanding and knowledge. It was in the public awareness and consciousness. This was not a hidden truth or occult. There was a masterful use of the knowledge. There were Rulers who understood the knowledge of the mastery of shape shifting. They had the knowledge and understanding of the symbolism of what you are referring to as the wolf.

NOTE: Herodotus was a Greek historian, born ca. 484 BC in Halicarnassus (modern day Turkey). He is known for his Magnus Opus "The Histories" which detailed the origins of the Greco-Persian Wars. In his writings he describes a tribe called the Neuri who "seemed to be magicians" and "changed once a year into wolves".

What can you tell us about the Neuri Tribe?

> The Neuri Tribe was aware that the death experience is a destruction of the form and the containment of the light. You are managing to avoid an involuntary disconnect experience or death when you shape shift. The Neuri Tribe practiced the energetic realignment and the direction and movement of the light between the containments. This is what Herodotus described and designated as a wolf-like form.

If the Neuri were capable of shape shifting why did they remain in the Earth plane?

> The Neuri were Sirius Beings who were trapped in the Earth plane existence but were further along in their mastery of time travel. Some however, were not actually bound to the Earth plane and chose to remain there in order to help other Beings who were trapped.

Are there others tribes currently existing on Earth that are like the Neuri and have remained to help us?

> There are tribes such as indigenous cultures who are voluntarily remaining in the Earth plane in order to help others achieve ascension experience. Many of you refer to these indigenous tribes as "caretakers of the Earth". They are actually caretakers of the light.

Are you suggesting that Earth is not worth caring for?

> This is not an accurate understanding. What we are bringing to your attention is that Earth has been created from the obstruction of the gateway. This belief will be further discussed in our next dialogue regarding Mithraism.

When did Mankind stop believing in the ability to shape shift?

> The understanding has been obstructed and grossly misappropriated since the linear historical date of 263 BC.

What occurred that caused this particular obstruction?

> There was an awareness that the knowledge of how to move the light and how to escape the Earth plane prison was being disseminated. The Rulers of the day made a decision to control the light and therefore control time as in controlling the ability to time travel.

Are you suggesting that the Rulers began controlling time by measuring it in a standardized way – as in the use of a sundial?

> Yes. The understanding that time was managed from this point forward is what must be absorbed. The understanding of how light can move was no longer available to the public. The public began to believe that the measure of the Sun – through the use of a sundial – was a beneficial institution, when in fact it was a manipulation of the truth. We will return to this discussion in your next Volume as it is beyond your Reader's rate of absorption.

You previously mentioned that shape shifting is the re-designation of energy and light in form? Why does the energy shift into a wolf form?

> Sirius is your origin and will be the first belief that most of you reconnect with when you make the disconnect experience. The Wolf Being symbolizes a reconnection with the Sirius star in your night sky, which is also known as the "Dog Star" through various mythologies and religions.

We are reconnecting with our origins, which have been associated with the Sirius Star and dog mythology.

> This is correct. The belief in Sirius, although somewhat forgotten, exists through metaphor and tales of wolves and wolf belief. It is still the overriding narrative across many civilizations in the Earth plane existence. The belief in Sirius and the Dog Star has not been completely forgotten. **When you make a disconnect experience and change your form, you will align with a form that you remember. The immediate belief is the existence of the Dog Star – Sirius.**

You said that the Wolf form is the first belief that most of us will reconnect with. Are you saying that some Sirius Beings might reconnect with a form other than the wolf?

> You do not need to subscribe to the belief in a wolf form. If you are expanding your belief protocol you may have a repertoire of other forms and containments.

Would the witness of a shape shift actually see us as a Wolf-Man?

> This is a question of perception. Witnesses have perceived the shape and experience as a Wolf Being or a Wolf State. You have constructed a mythology and a story around this experience. It is most unfortunate that the wolf has become associated with a widely spread tale of fear. It should be a point of curiosity to you all, that the majority of you fear the ascension experience. You have all experienced the fear of running with the wolves.

Does this mean that Beings who are not of Sirius origin will shape shift into another animal or form other than the wolf?

> This is a correct understanding. You will soon understand and absorb that as you are learning the time travel experience you will reconnect with other beliefs that you have forgotten. Some of these beliefs are narratives and symbols that are hidden in plain sight. We are speaking of the many existing folklores and mythologies that describe the man/beast metaphor.

We'd like to detail some specific mythologies for the Reader.

> There is an important analogy and explanation regarding the wolf mythology and folklore. Please refer to what you are calling the Capitoline Wolf sculpture.

NOTE: The founding of Ancient Rome is told through the legend of twin brothers Romulus and Remus. The brothers were cast into the Tiber River and later rescued and cared for by a she-wolf. The Capitoline Wolf is a bronze sculpture depicting a scene from the legend in which the twin brothers suckle their wolf mother (research image before reading).

What do the twins represent in this wolf sculpture?

> One twin represents the connection most of you have with your 3rd density Earth experience. The other sibling in the twin pair represents the connection with the Other World. This is the dual connection and experiences that are important in order for you to thoroughly realign your belief. You

> cannot make a change unless you can contain the belief in more than two places at one "time".

Please elaborate.

> What we are suggesting is that the twins are the representation that you must consider yourself as being in a pair, for the initial reformation of belief. This is the beginning of the understanding that wolf symbolism and the wolf experience is a vehicle of information.

This sculpture and depiction is essentially representing our reconnection with Lyra and the world just beyond it. Is this an accurate understanding?

> This is correct. The sculpture is a symbol of the understanding and belief in the Intermediary World. It also represents the belief that this understanding and knowledge was never lost. It was hoarded and concealed. There are many of you that continue your understanding and therefore continue your experience and continue your travel.

It feels as though we are being taunted by the exhibition and display of this statue – this is just another example of the truth hiding in plain sight.

> The making of the statue is not a taunt. The decision to hoard the meaning was and is a decision that was based on power and authority. The organization in place decided that the naiveté of the masses would be the agreed upon existence.

In Werewolf folklore, the transformation occurs during a full moon. What is this event representing?

> There was once a belief that shape shifting would allow one to become closer to a luminary. The existence of the knowledge was contained in a respectable belief stream. Put into practice these beliefs allowed you to reconnect with your true condition as a Light Being.

Were people not frightened at the sight of a shape shift?

> The understanding that the light is contained in the forms that you now consider dark or dreadful and invoke fear has created an unfortunate belief where you fear yourselves. The things that frighten you the most are those things that you will benefit from.

Many of us are frightened by even the slightest variance within our own species. Our fear of most other forms seems to be a default human trait.

> There is more than one physical expression of the light and the light containment. Your readers must redevelop and reacquaint themselves with the understanding that not all forms appear as youthful as Man Being. The understanding that there are grotesque and scary things that you must run from and be afraid of is an inaccuracy. You are running away from your own innate abilities.

Our fear of the non-human form runs deep. This may be a difficult concept for readers to absorb.

MAN BEING

> You do not travel through the densities of experience as a perfectly formed Man Being. Many of you equate your experience of ascension with being in an angelic realm. You believe your "afterlife" is contained in the experience of a humanoid or Man Being form – but elevated. This is not an accurate belief.

We take on other forms while we reassemble our Light Body. Is this correct?

> This is accurate. There are many forms and not all are recognizable. There is a density of experience where you will experience the physical form of a Being that you will call a Wolf Being or Wolf-like Being. Those things that you are fearful of and run away in horror from are actually your own Being. You must reacquaint yourselves with this truth. The luminaries are responsible for helping you move the light, as you are also responsible for moving the luminaries. The light moves and so does the containment in form in and out of the densities of experience.

Our understanding of the Moon's function and our relationship to it is very limited. You are describing the Moon as an integral component of the ascension journey.

> The Moon is not simply a gravitational facilitator or an ornament as many of you are choosing to believe. The luminosities and the luminaries change and shift and re-equate themselves with your experience of understanding and your experience of belief. When you shift your idea and you shift how you contain your idea and you shift how you form

the containment of your idea, then your belief is also contained and shifted in Lyra.

Is shape shifting referenced in our Bible books?

The expression of the "wolf in sheep's clothing" is used in your Bible books. This simple understanding will best inform your readers.

NOTE: The New Testament Book of Matthew is perhaps the most quoted use of the expression. The following passage is taken from Matthew Chapter 7, verse 15.

"Beware the false prophets, who come to you in sheep's clothing but inwardly are ravenous wolves".

The wolf is an antagonist in this passage. Why is it presented this way?

The devouring of a belief or a belief system is a frightening or a threatening perception for those who are antiquated in their beliefs. This is the common perception for those who do not have the capacity to reconnect to new beliefs – which are in fact old beliefs that they must reassemble.

The use of this expression seems to be a deliberate hijacking of our connection to the wolf and the shape shifting experience.

This is a correct assessment. The sheep, as in the masses and the unaware, are the Beings who need to make a reconnection before a disconnection. Then there are many who are in a disconnected state but not in a released state. This is represented in the Shepherd.

Please elaborate on that point.

> There are many tales in different cultures of Shepherds leading flocks. This is an important understanding for you to absorb as this allegory and demonstration is repeated across many different cultural civilizations and truths. There is a Shepherd that leads and there is a wolf that devours. The wolf devours the out-dated existence and paradigm of belief in order to disconnect and release. The meaning of this tale has been twisted in the sense that you now admonish wolf behaviour and protect the sheep that remain in the state of unawareness.

This is such a simple tale and yet we've managed to misinterpret the meaning.

> There are Beings who are making changes and sudden changes of disconnect ability, as in the story of the wolf attacking. Fear of the wolf is a fear of ascension experience. The wolf as a symbol of fear and terror is what must be corrected.

How can we best articulate the correction?

> The wolf represents the motion of the ability to reassemble beliefs in a new shape and a new place of understanding – this is shape shifting.

Are there mythologies that use different creatures to represent the same experience?

> There are many. There is one in particular that is well known albeit incorrectly attributed to the civilization known as Greece. You must designate

the legend of the Minotaur to a new civilization and understanding.

NOTE: The Minotaur in Greek mythology was a hybrid creature, half man half bull. When King Minos of Crete refused to sacrifice the bull to Poseidon (God of the Sea), Poseidon caused the King's wife to lust after the animal. They conceived the Minotaur who was eventually imprisoned in a Labyrinth and killed by the hero Theseus.

What civilization was responsible for this legend?

> There was a civilization that arrived and settled along the Tyrrhenian Sea in the geographic location you now call Italy. We are speaking to you about the people known as the Etruscans.

NOTE: The Etruscans were a civilization situated in ancient Italy ca. 900 BC. They were largely populated in the area corresponding to modern day Tuscany but also reached as far North as Veneto and as South as Campania.

Why is it important to correct this?

> Etruscan Beings brought the knowledge about shape shifting. The origin of the Minotaur and the origin of the Werewolf are one in the same story.

What can you tell us about the Minotaur story?

> The Minotaur is an understanding that we are reassembling the form. It is the understanding and belief that there is an intermediary stage between form, disconnect and reform. The understanding that in order to pursue the origin and the next phase

> in your existence, through time travel and the connection with Lyra, there will need to be a re-modification of form.

The Minotaur was also depicted as abhorrent and was given seven sacrificial humans to devour.

> This fear mongering has steered you all away from your ability to change form. The Minotaur represents the state of being during the change. Much like the understanding of the shape shifting Wolf-Man, the Minotaur is an experience in the understanding that time travel requires and equates to a new form.

How are these truths so easily hijacked and concealed? It's difficult to accept that we're so easily manipulated.

> The explanation is simple but one that Man Being continues to reject. The Rulers of the day were in direct contact and connection with these truths and chose power and control over dissemination. The truth about the experience in shape shifting was reformatted and edited in a way to incorrectly disseminate the truth. This is the reason why you have lost your way.

Will readers struggle to accept that we will not always be in human form?

> It is essential for all of you to continue believing and reconnecting with your ability to move in and out of your form. The understanding that your form is not the only form that you will experience is something that you must equate with respect. The forms that

will benefit you in the time travel experience are forms of physicality that you admonished or are fearful of. Your history and folklore and mythologies contain incorrect truths. They are created to scare and impose a fear of the unknown and a fear of anything but your form as Human in the Earth plane.

Why do we take on new forms – aren't we supposed to be reassembling a Light Body? Or are these forms simply an expression of the light?

The time travel experience requires containment in form. You must learn about the different shapes and sounds and containments of physical form in order for the light to be able to move through the densities. The next level of experience will be the form that you are referring to as a wolf form.

To clarify, we only take forms to contain the light for travel but we are ultimately Beings of Light. Is this correct?

This is an accurate understanding. You must recognize the allowance to move the light and move the form. You see a Wolf Being because there is a change in form and that form is similar to what you are describing as a wolf. You see in form because you are in form now. You must be in form in order to see another form. You will reach a place and space where you are also able to see the light and see yourself in light. You will no longer need to exist in a form if you choose to contain the light in a place where light exists freely.

Information about the Octopus and Sea Creatures in Volume 1 resonated with many readers. Is this the recognition of our own latent abilities?

> There is an ability for you to morph into a new form. Your form will be way beyond your belief about what can happen to your physical body as you are seeing it now. There is a transformation that can and will take place and you must be prepared for this experience so that you do not misinterpret it in a negative light.

What final message can you share with the Reader about the shape shifting experience?

> In order to make a correct journey there is a series of necessary formations and reformations. The entry into other worlds is through the gateway of your beliefs. Lyra is the preparation for this journey. You are making your homeward journey and the travel is not in a spaceship or "UFO". The travel is in your own spaceship of many different forms and reforms. Please accept that this dialogue is the beginning of a new belief that has already been accepted and practiced by many of your so-called ancient and tribal cultures and peoples.

Will we be discussing in depth any of those cultures or practices?

> We will discuss the practices and beliefs of what you are calling Mithraic Mysteries.

3

Mithras

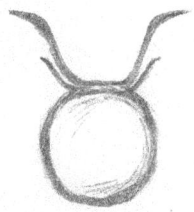

NOTE: Mithras was a deity that appeared in the Roman Empire during the 1st century AD. Several hundred Mithraeum (temples to Mithras) have been found across Europe, North Africa and the Middle East. The Mithraeum is a narrow cavern that seated approximately 30 members, men only. A statue or painting of Mithras slaying a bull, called a Tauroctony, was typically placed at the front of the room and also included depictions of other animals.

What can you tell us about Mithras?

> There is a specific discussion with regards to the Mithras information and specific knowledge of Lyra that is being hidden in the Vatican Library. The available information that is being hidden in the library will shed insights into how long the concealment has been contained.

Will the Vatican's stockpile of concealed information ever be revealed to the public?

> The understanding that Mithraic knowledge and information has been suppressed for an extended period of time will result in an unprecedented amount of questions and controversy. There will be further collapse of infrastructure as Beings wish to learn more.

What can we share about Mithras that isn't already known to scholars?

> This was once a teaching about ascension and ascension experience that allowed a direct access to Lyra. The experience of the release of the Light Body was not something that was an esoteric or

hidden belief. This was part of a belief system and understanding that everyone involved had access to.

Historians believe that Mithraism was practiced in the Roman Empire from the 1st to 4th century AD. Are these dates accurate?

> Mithras was widespread up until the time period of the Jesus experience. Mithraism was in fact a thriving civilization that resulted in the experience of the Lemuria state. The Mithras "cults" your historians are referring to in the linear dates of the 1st to 4th century AD were imitation experiences.

What exactly do you mean by imitation experiences?

> The underground movement or cults that you are describing that supposedly existed during these linear dates are associated with Beings who had already forgotten the knowledge. They were struggling to recreate the experience through imitation ritual. The true assembly of Mithraism, as you refer to it, was widespread up until the Jesus experience.

NOTE: There were 7 grades of initiation that members underwent throughout their participation in the Mithraic rituals. The initiates could be promoted to each new level if their peers judged them worthy.

Did these Mithraic teachings originate in Sumer or Rome?

> These beliefs and practices originated near the area known as the Euphrates River. The origin and the civilization is not as important as the understanding

that the specific concepts and beliefs were eventually corrupted and twisted into some of the practices that you are involved in today.

In what way have we corrupted the Mithraic concepts?

> The creation of your modern Legal System comes from the concept of being judged when you "cross over". Your legal system is a reflection of your misunderstanding of the experience in Lyra and the experience in the involuntary disconnect. When you are not prepared, you interpret the Beings in Lyra and in the involuntary disconnect experience as your Adjudicators.

Is our Legal System also based on the initiation rituals and peer approval?

> Yes and these rituals were also a failed attempt to resurrect the original Mithraic experience. Mithras was an ascension teaching. Your civilization however, is working away from the light. This was not the intention of the Mithras teachings.

If these Mithraic rituals were such a key influence on our current legal and social framework, why do we know very little about them?

> There is a control of the information release. There is a delay when there is a discovery. Not all of the discoveries are shared in a beneficial timing. Please be assured that when there are accounts of archaeological findings and new understandings about history that these are not necessarily new

findings. They are simply findings that are being allowed to be released.

Why release the information at all if the agenda is to conceal?

> Information is released when a belief structure collapses. "Discoveries" are made when Beings en masse request that the information be released. The Man Being book dissemination is creating a monumental and global demand for access to information. You will see.

Why were women not allowed to attend the Mithraeum?

> Women already had the knowledge and did not need to participate. They were not excluded from the participation as they were already making the ascension experience.

Why were women already in possession of the knowledge?

> Women were leaders in the ascension experience and dissemination. They were once held in high regard, such that their beliefs and their understanding about the Mithras experience and ascension knowledge was widely accepted.

Are you speaking of the priestesses who would administer religious rite and practice in the temples?

> Yes. Women had the role and assumed dissemination responsibility through lyric and the playing of music in the temples. This responsibility was taken away from them and they were relegated to being audience members instead of contributors

> to the teaching of ascension. Their voices were effectively quieted, as they were no longer permitted to use these instruments to play and sing for the purpose of dissemination.

Where and during what time period did the suppression begin?

> This experience began in southern Greece, as the laws gradually changed between the 4th and 3rd centuries BC. We are speaking of the oracles. The male teachers took the responsibility away from the priestesses. They effectively changed the meaning of the teachings and placed it in a different stream of understanding. This was not a sudden change, as it was completed over many linear years.

We are using the ancient terms "priestess" and "oracle" but we are effectively describing psychics – people who are modified with the ability to connect with other streams of consciousness.

> This is correct. The women who had the ability were not a special group of Beings. There was a time in your linear history when all women had this ability and were encouraged to share their understanding. The women in your Earth plane existence today who have this ability are undoubtedly connected with these "ancient" priestesses. The ability to see and know and understand is an innate ability as you are all aware. In this case however, all women had the ability to connect and reconnect with the belief in ascension.

Will this information help to reignite female interest in ascension?

> This is what you are transmitting in Volume 2, as it is necessary in the ascension experience that women once again assume their role and position. They must contribute to the ascension experience en masse. They must once again share what they all know. They are carrying knowledge from previous incarnation streams that is now of use and needed in order for you to make the homeward journey. **The belief in Lyra is a fundamental belief that all women share. They all have the innate ability to reconnect to the Lyra experience with minimal modification.**

Why do all women have the innate ability to connect?

> The ability for the Light Body containment is greater in the Beings you are referring to as female. This is not a question of one "gender" being smarter or better in ascension experience than another. The light that is contained in the Earth plane female is directed specifically toward ascension experience. The light contained in the Earth plane male is directed toward experience and accumulation of experience. This is a demonstration of active and passive energy. These are the noted differences in the characteristics between many male and female Beings in the Earth plane.

Many male psychics exist today. Does that mean that they were female Beings in a previous incarnation?

> Males that are experiencing the psychic ability and intuitive quality that you are speaking about have already had a reconnection experience – in a previous incarnation. They do not necessarily have to have experienced incarnations as a female. Your readers will ask if they too need to connect with their own innate "psychic" ability in order to reconnect. This is not the case. You simply need to be exposed to the signal and the transmission.

There is currently another energy that is being described as "non-binary" or "non-gender". What is being expressed through this experience?

> These Beings have adjusted their beliefs. They are refusing to contain themselves in one energy designation versus another so that they are not defining themselves as either a male or female. They have begun to integrate the experience, albeit unconsciously in most cases. The Earth plane existence is also not a convenient one for these Beings. It is difficult for them to make this leap in belief, as there is not a paradigm that will welcome this belief stream.

The energetic qualities of each gender contribute to a belief stream. Is that what you're saying?

> This is accurate. The adjustment in the type of light and the light source is what you are asking about for light is not graded in good or bad or levels of

beneficial experience. Light is integrated in a way that allows belief streams to manifest.

What you're ultimately saying is that the male and female energies have to unite in order to ascend.

> This is a simplified understanding. The belief streams of the female energy containment versus the male energy containment are very different in the Earth plane experience. This is your challenge. The reintegration of energies must occur in order for a beneficial assembly of beliefs toward ascension. You must all come together for the release of the Light Body and the homeward journey.

You've mentioned how females are reconnecting with Lyra. How are males achieving the reconnection?

> The Male Being in the 3rd density Earth plane existence is different in that his reconnections and beliefs must be experienced. Once the reconnection is made, males will drive the ascension experience. They will encourage females to once again contribute and lead the experience of 2034. They will encourage females to resurrect the Mithraic teachings.

We'd like to discuss the teachings in detail. Why is Mithras depicted slaying a bull?

> The depiction of Mithras slaying the bull, as in the Tauroctony, is communicating how you are being taught to kill the light. The slaying of a bull is representing a complete shut down in the belief that you may change your physical form. The belief that

one must slay and one must fear these mythological creatures is the reason why you continue on a self-destructive path.

The depiction of Mithras slaying the bull is telling us what not to do – is that correct?

> This is an accurate understanding. You must understand that the form must reform and that your form is a fluid experience, as we have already discussed with regards to shape shifting.

It is believed that bulls were sacrificed in the Mithraeum. Is this true?

> The sacrificing of a bull pertains to the imitation cults that we are speaking about. They assumed that a practice of sacrifice was a way to somehow access the light and the light codes in order to fix what was broken or missing in their existing Light Body. Consumption of other Beings is somewhat an attempt to repair a broken Light Body. This is ineffective.

To clarify, animal sacrifice is not an effective way to repair our broken Light Bodies or absorb light code.

> The complete experience of the Light Body release does not require the forced disconnect or sacrifice of another Being. Those that have achieved the real knowledge do not need to participate and bring other Beings with them in a mandated physical release of another Being's Light Body. Animal sacrifice was an ineffective imitation ritual. It is the disconnect and the releasing of the light codes that

many of you were seeking to imitate through animal sacrifice.

Is that the main reason why the Ancients practiced animal sacrifice?

> This is correct. The bull is an allegory and a representation of the voluntary disconnect and the release of the Light Body. The bull represents light. Animal sacrifice was a misconception and a misunderstanding. There was a desperate need and a search for the experience and the tools that some Beings had and continue to have.

Why is the bull a symbol of light?

> The apex of this belief is integrated with the luminary and the constellation.

Are you referring to the Taurus constellation?

> Yes. The luminary or constellation is created and represented in form, in the Earth plane existence. There are many Beings, such as the bull, existing in the Earth plane that are recreations or representations of your belief.

What belief are you referring to?

> We are speaking of the belief in your existence in light. The luminaries are created from beliefs and these beliefs are represented in the Earth plane.

This is extraordinary. Our beliefs create the stars and these constellations manifest in physical form on Earth – e.g. a bull from the Taurus constellation.

> You will learn more about this in Volumes 3 and 4. Many of you are beginning to reformat your belief and therefore be flexible in your understanding of the constellations. You are all beginning to demonstrate a belief in the light and in the creation of light. There was once a time when many of you felt connected with the constellations. The constellations therefore created a belief. In this case, that belief exists as a bull. The bull is a creature that is representing a belief and therefore is existing in the ascension experience.

Our beliefs created life forms on Earth. As outrageous as that may seem, the science isn't yet concrete on how Earth's complex life forms came to be.

NOTE: Scientists believe that somewhere around 900 million years ago, single celled organisms (microbes) began living inside other microbes. It is unclear as to how or why this happened. These multi-celled organisms were the forerunners to complex life on earth.

> You have created the Beings that you are interacting with. You have created a bull, as you believe in the constellation of the bull. You believe in the creation of the light that comes from this constellation. You are aware that in ascension you make light and use light.

This is a major shift in belief.

> There is an assumption that the Earth is creating life. This is not a correct understanding. You are creating life. The rock that you are existing on is a creation from your beliefs that you are stuck in form. Please ensure that you are explaining this concept, as your readers will need to prepare and adjust their belief about what they are referring to as "Mother Earth".

You refer to Earth as the rock that we exist on. Mithras is depicted emerging from a rock. What does this symbolize?

> The rock represents the formation of a luminary, such as a planet in 3rd density experience.

Mithras is escaping this rock.

> This represents the escape from the entrapment in the fixed plane and the fixed grid. A rock is a fixed understanding and an entrapment. Mithras is the freeing of this experience and the return to the world of freeform existence.

The Tauractony and Mithraeum commonly included depictions of ancillary animals and Zodiac symbols. The animals were typically a dog, serpent, scorpion, raven and lion. What were they representing?

> As we have already discussed, the wolf form is a stage in the movement of your Light Body. The different animal forms and astrological attributes that you are describing are different stages in the Light Body movement. There are different forms that you can access and recreate. The understanding that the shape of Man Being is the

representation of God in the highest form is not the correct understanding. Your light can enter different states of consciousness that are equated with different forms and forms of existence.

We are stuck on the idea that the human anatomy or form is the ultimate construction.

> You are all "stuck". Nature is a gateway to your understanding of the truth that form is not encapsulating you, but you are encapsulating it. This knowledge is part of a monumental reveal that will be discussed in a later chapter – regarding a hidden truth about your planet. Please continue with your questions about the Mithraeum.

What occurred during a typical congregation at the original Mithraeum (not the imitation cults)?

> The Mithraeum was a meeting of the minds and a meeting of the network. This was a reassembly and a reconnection among those Beings who are ascending in a Soul Ascension Group.

Did they do this unconsciously or did people of the same group knowingly convene in this way?

> What you are describing may seem like an allegory when in fact this is the actual experience. You are describing the ascension experience en masse. You are not describing the individual rituals that are reported in the archaeological and historical disseminations.

The Mithraeum were designated locations where Beings and Soul Assembly Groups could experience a mass ascension.

> There are elements of truth to the Mithras journey and experience and there are elements of cheap ritual and imitation. Please make the distinction for your readers.

The Mithraic cults from the 1st to 4th century AD were the imitation cults who had incomplete knowledge.

> This is a correct understanding. These were Beings who had already left the Church and left the Abrahamic religions and secretly wished for the understanding and the return homeward. These Beings had accumulated an interest en masse in retreating from the structure and the civilization but did not have the complete skills or mastery. These are seekers of knowledge and they were of Sirius origin in their undertaking.

The Mithraeum caverns that archaeologists have discovered were built by this group who reverted to cheap ritual. Is that correct?

> Yes. These were Beings who recognized that they were in fact left behind but did not understand the parameters or the complete story about ascension. There were attempts to discover how to reconnect and there were attempts to reassemble their Light Body and there were attempts to release their Light Body through ritualistic practices. You are speaking about the shadows or remnants of the actual ascension experience.

To clarify, there were Beings who attended the earlier Mithraeum and released their Light body.

> Yes, at a linear place and space in your historical account that is much earlier than the 1st century AD. The places and spaces in your linear history you are inquiring about as in the later years after Jesus are incorrect. These are imitations of the experiences that were no longer achievable.

How far back into linear time do we have to reference to cite a successful disconnect and release via Mithraic practice?

> The battle in 163 BC involving Judah Maccabee and the linear years that led up to this place and space were a battle to conceal the knowledge. Once Beings receive the knowledge and have the knowledge and achieve the ascension, other Beings will also achieve the knowledge and ascension. Once ascension begins other Beings will also ascend. This is how belief systems collapse and this is why the knowledge is repeatedly supressed and concealed.

Is it accurate to say that a civilization springs from the knowledge of ascension?

> The understanding that there is a continued evolution of culture and beliefs along a linear timeline is inaccurate. An ascension event shapes a culture and the events that occur afterward are all depictions of some form of suppression and some form of diminishing of the light.

Are we reviving Mithras with this dissemination?

Yes. You are essentially entering a Mithras age. There is a search for knowledge and a search for restitution as your ability to release the Light Body is your birthright. Mithras did not die out. Your ability to understand it did. What you must turn your attention toward now is the Source of your Light

4

Go to the Light

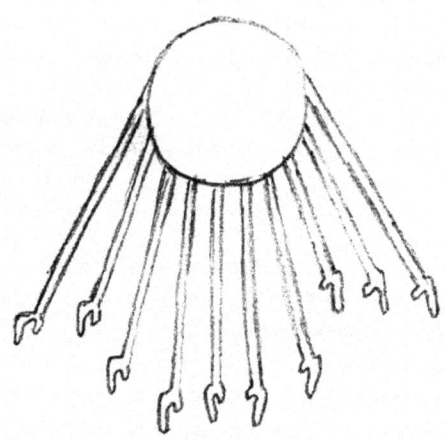

You've mentioned that we must turn our attention to the "Source of our Light"? What is the Source of our Light?

> In order to understand and absorb this information you must revisit and redefine the death experience or what we are calling the involuntary disconnect.

In what way can we redefine the death experience?

> There is a dilemma for those of you who lack the preparation for the death experience or what we are calling the involuntary disconnect. There is some difficulty in the involuntary disconnect when one attempts to reassemble their truths and their beliefs in a very hurried manner. This creates a decision to reassemble in the reincarnation cycle.

You mentioned in Volume 1 that when we "die" we experience something that we don't understand and we therefore choose reincarnation instead of immortality.

> This is correct. What is lacking in the general awareness of the Near Death Experience or NDE is that the "tunnel of light" is a place where you are meeting other Beings – like you – who are forming their Light Bodies. Their assembly is creating the experience of the light that is being witnessed in the NDE.

What will our readers need to know about this "tunnel" experience?

> The understanding that there are assembled Beings is the first step to help and assist those that find

themselves suddenly in the Intermediary World of Lyra – and do not know how to navigate.

Who exactly are these assembled "Beings" that you're referring to?

There are many of you waiting and building the Light Body and these are the Beings we are speaking of. The acceptance and the understanding that you are not alone in this Intermediary World is information that is needed. This understanding will help you make the correct decision and not choose the reincarnation cycle.

Is there a specific question that is posed to us in the tunnel or involuntary disconnect experience? Is there a specific Being doing the asking?

You will be asked if you would like to join us.

If it's that simple why are Beings reincarnating?

There is a fear of joining an assembly of Light Beings that appear strange to you. This is the dilemma that is being dealt with incorrectly. The fact is that this is all part of a soul ascension experience. The soul ascension experience is a containment of a multitude of Beings, some of which you may know in your 3rd density Earth plane experience and some of which you may not be aware of. The assembly of Beings is required in order to make the journey to the next world beyond Lyra. This is what you must prepare for.

To clarify, we continue to reject the assembly of Beings in Lyra in favor of the Earth plane existence – which is actually a prison state.

> This is correct. Confronted with the choice there is an immediate panic and request to join your "loved ones" on Earth again. This is a most unfortunate experience as we are all waiting to make the ascension journey together in a collective union of light experience.

Why is this not being explained to us in the disconnect experience? Why leave it to such a vague proposition?

> This information is shared. What is not happening is the processing of the information, as you are conditioned to prefer the Earth plane existence and the entrapment cycle. The "proposition" that we bring to you in this dialogue is simplified for this discussion. There is an exchange of codes and information that occurs in the involuntary disconnect experience or the NDE.

Is the information so jarring that we can't compute the experience?

> Yes. Beings must have prior knowledge before being exposed to this experience. There is not enough interest in the involuntary disconnect experience and therefore not enough preparation. This is not a matter of us not sharing or discussing the options. This is simply your lack of experience with ascension. Experience with ascension tools will enable you to absorb and process the information

that is being shared in the involuntary disconnect and near death experience.

It's still difficult to imagine that we would choose reincarnation in the presence of Light and a World of Immortality.

> The truth is that many of you are afraid of contact with the Light Beings in Lyra – because you perceive them as disfigured or grotesque. From this simple fear many of you choose the reincarnation cycle over the cycle of immortality.

Why do we perceive them as disfigured or grotesque?

> You are all reassembling in light. You do not yet understand the process of the Light Body reassembly. You fear what you do not understand.

How can we help to quell that fear for the Reader?

> The understanding that Lyra is a place to make the reconnections and prepare for further travel is what is missing in the understanding. It is this simple truth that will assist those who are encountering a sudden connection with our World. It is a sudden connection with our World that you are running from. You have in fact made the journey and can have a successful ascension experience. Involuntary disconnect or "death" does not have to be problematic if you are aware that Lyra exists.

Both Dramos and I have had similar visions recently. We believe that we're being shown something that exists in the "tunnel experience". What are we witnessing?

Please describe your visions for the readers.

DRAMOS' VISION: It is the blackest of black. Something gigantic emerges from the darkness that has a pinkish under glow. Its torso looks like a tree trunk. It has no limbs and a large head with no face. White strands of light extend out from the face in thick cords like a sea anemone. I sense that it is aware of my presence.

BOHEMIAS' VISION: I see a gigantic pitch-black spherical Being – I'm not sure what it is. Extending from it are many cords of electric-blue light that flicker intermittently. It feels to me like a generator and looks a bit like Tesla's coil.

> What you have both experienced is an encounter with the channel of light. For ease of understanding you may refer to this as "The Channel" from this point forward. This is what Akhenaten referred to as the "Aten". Beings who choose the involuntary disconnect will experience this encounter in the "tunnel", as you refer to it.

NOTE: See the Chapter 4 drawing for a depiction of Akhenaten's Aten. The Aten was a symbol for what Pharaoh Akhenaten (born ca. 1380 BC) believed was the Source of all Light. It was represented as a sun-disc with rays ending in outstretched hands.

What is this Being?

> The understanding of The Channel has been hijacked and disseminated in a twisted and bizarre way so that the Source of your Light is now feared.

We encounter the Source of our Light in the tunnel experience and react in fear. We can refer to this Being as "The Channel". Is this correct?

> Yes. You are afraid of yourselves and afraid of your origin and afraid of your origin story and this correction will be made and provided for in this dissemination. Most of you experience fear or apprehension when exposed to The Channel.

This is not what most of us would expect to encounter in the "afterlife".

> You are expecting that there are Beings who are similar to your form, as in the Earth plane form. You have been depicting angels like Man Being but with wings and built more in light. These are not correct understandings or beliefs – not for this stage in the disconnect experience and immersion in Lyra.

Readers will likely find this bizarre.

> Your readers will need to understand that these are descriptions of what you are ultimately becoming.

Are you saying that we're turning into gigantic spheres of light?

> This is not correct. What you are witnessing and becoming is a Being who is able to generate its own light.

Why does one vision describe a tree trunk while the other doesn't?

> You will have a clearer understanding once we discuss the symbolism of the Tree of Life. Both of your visions of The Channel represent how you initially generate your light. From this event, you are able to create experiences whereby you may exist in more than one density of experience – as you make the ascension journey.

Why haven't people described The Channel in their near death experiences?

> Some of you have experienced The Channel or Tesla ball, as you are describing. You are not able to integrate the experience as you are fixed in your 3rd density consciousness. This is the main reason and explanation why it is not a widely disseminated and shared experience. You believe that what you have experienced is an incorrect belief. Angels and Beings of Light in human form are the accepted belief and the belief that most of you have integrated into your consciousness.

The problem is that we are experiencing a higher frequency or state of being while holding firm to our 3rd density beliefs. Is that correct?

> Yes. In the tunnel experience you are experiencing the remnant of your 3rd density consciousness integrated into a timeless factor of experience. These two are overlapping and intersecting so that you are unable to process a new belief in the 5th density or in this tunnel experience. You are experiencing "the tunnel of light" without the proper preparation and so The Channel is not a concept that you can easily absorb or disseminate upon your "return".

Most people who describe their NDE claim that they were instructed to return to Earth because it was "not their time". Why are they describing other Beings making the decision for them?

> In the tunnel of light you are encountering what happens when you are suddenly exposed to a massive amount of light without the knowledge and awareness. Beings that are being exposed to the light are not able to process the light. They do not have the ability to contain the light and so there is a feeling of a lack of control. Most of you are "blinded by the light" and hold onto your 3rd density belief systems. The understanding that you have been relieved of this experience and "sent back" as it is "not your time" is the justification that you are asking about.

People have stated clearly that their loved ones met them in the tunnel and told them to return to Earth. How can we mistake our family members?

> The descriptions of "relatives" ushering you back to Earth is not a correct understanding, for you make the decision alone. The Beings who are experiencing the NDE are not lying – they simply do not understand what is actually occurring. This is somewhat of an advanced discussion that we will continue preparing you for in your instruction of what to do in the involuntary disconnect experience.

How has The Channel been so concealed from Mankind?

> You have created a history and a story that has been absorbed through many different cultures. Your

mythologies have convinced you that the encounter with The Channel and Source of your Light causes death. You have all chosen to believe that the source of your creation is also the end. You have created an awareness that the light brings death and that the approach to the Being from which you are all created is a death experience. This understanding has been a hideous obstacle for you all.

Is Akhenaten's Aten an appropriate portrayal of The Channel? Our visions seemed more lifelike and imposing by comparison.

> The Channel is equated with Akhenaten's Aten disc. Please remember that your perceptions may vary but the concept is the same. The Aten is a similar portrayal of this energy.

Do we also encounter The Channel if we are making the voluntary disconnect?

> The encounter occurs exclusively in the involuntary death experience. Those Beings who are making the voluntary disconnect experience are already embracing this "Being" as the Source of the Light and the Source of the Energy. This Being may be equated with a female aspect in order for you to better understand that the Source of your Being and your existence has been created and provided for by this Being.

If the Channel is the Source of our Light and Energy, where does that leave our Sun?

> The Channel has provided you the light source and the energy for your existence. This truth has been obscured through tales of the Sun and Moon ruling your lives. You in fact rule the Sun and Moon. The origin of the light is not from the physical Sun and Moon or from the stars and the planets. Light travel and light reassembly is experienced when you encounter The Channel – who is providing channels of light.

This is quite the revelation. What else do we need to understand about The Channel?

> Please assure your readers that they will receive "first hand" accounts of encounters with The Channel – in Volume 3. The encounter with The Channel is essentially your doorway into Lyra. It is a doorway you have forgotten about but are now reconnecting with. Please regard this as a doorway or gateway at this place in the dialogue.

Is The Channel specific to Sirius Beings?

> Beings of Sirius origin make up this Energy Source and you are assembling yourselves in this way as you create portals through the time gradients. The Channel is the Source of your Light. Beings that belong to other Soul Ascension Groups will learn of their origins through their own Ascension Events. Please remember that you are disseminating this information for the benefit of Sirius Beings. The others will organize themselves as you are doing here. We have already made clear that if you are reading and absorbing the information in the Man Being dissemination then you are of Sirius origin.

You've said that stories about the danger of this Being have been disseminated in order to discourage us to return homeward. Please give us an example.

The Medusa figure has been equated with The Channel in a most unfortunate way. Please refer to your stories of Perseus and the Medusa figure, as this is a correct comparison.

NOTE: In Greek mythology, Perseus is the son of Zeus and Danae. Perseus is ordered by a King to behead one of the Gorgon sisters, named Medusa. Medusa's hair was made of living serpents and her stare would turn anyone who looked at her to stone.

What is our current understanding of this myth?

> The Medusa figure is equated with the Channel or Source of your Light. Your understanding that Perseus must slay the Medusa and take her head reinforces the belief and decision to no longer exist in the form that you originated in.

How can we correct this understanding?

> The serpents on Medusa's head are a representation of the light, as in cords of light. The serpents are equivalent to light. The serpentine head symbolizes the enlightened state, unobstructed from knowledge. Your understanding that snakes or serpents represent evil is a misaligned belief. You must not slay the Medusa, but become her.

In the myth, Perseus must avoid looking at the Medusa so that he does not turn to stone. What is the meaning of turning to stone?

> This is a reminder that you are all accepting your physical form as the penultimate form. You are all accepting yourselves as stone rather than light. This allegory is describing how you stopped believing that you are light bearers and light bringers and light generators.

Essentially, we must look directly at the Medusa and not avoid her.

> Yes. Look directly at this belief and absorb this understanding. You are not trapped in a physical form. You do not die from accepting the belief that you can and will generate your own light. It is light that you are bringing into your lives. Release yourselves from the Earth prison. Release the prison.

In the story, Perseus maneuvers around the Medusa using a mirror in his shield – so that he can avoid her stare. Why doesn't Perseus look at the Medusa if we are supposed to embrace what she represents?

> He is the bearer of truth. Perseus is the Messenger in this story. You are all being asked to look at yourselves. The story has been manipulated and misunderstood but the presentation of ideas is quite clear.

Are you suggesting that because Perseus has already accepted the beliefs, he doesn't need to look at the Medusa to become Immortal or survive death?

> This is correct. Perseus' adventure is representing the involuntary disconnect experience. He is showing you what you will experience in the involuntary disconnect. You must embrace The Channel – the Source of your Light. Do not fear yourselves.

Is this book series equivalent to Perseus' journey?

> Yes. You are holding up the book for your readers as Perseus held up the head. You are bringing a new belief to reconnect with. You are bringing the understanding that you must look at yourself. We are not suggesting that you look at yourselves inwardly, as many of you might be inclined to interpret.

Are you saying to look at The Channel head on?

> Yes. If you are experiencing the involuntary disconnect you must face what you are calling The Channel head on. The involuntary disconnect is an opportunity for you to look at yourselves as this is the chance for you to see yourself in a fully formed Light Being state. Go to the light and reassemble your Light Body in Lyra.

In Volume 1 you urged us to encourage readers to choose the voluntary disconnect path. We want to remind readers that we don't have to experience death if we choose to voluntarily disconnect.

> This is correct. Those Beings who are able to achieve a voluntary disconnect experience do not need to encounter The Channel, as they are already fully formed and accept this experience. Those Beings who are not able to reassemble their beliefs and reconnections while they are experiencing the Earth existence will encounter The Channel – and must accept this belief.

For readers who haven't read Volume 1, please describe the two paths.

> You have an opportunity to process new beliefs in layers and absorb and prepare for ascension – this is the voluntary disconnect. By voluntarily disconnecting you are creating a Light Body and you will not experience death, as you know it. If you do not prepare for ascension in your "lifetime" on Earth, you will experience death via illness or circumstance – this is the involuntary disconnect. In this experience you will be confronted with a seemingly "terrifying" experience, as you have a lack of preparation. The involuntary disconnect is the choice that most of you make and fail at, as the prospect of facing The Channel is something that you cannot manage or absorb.

Choose to voluntarily disconnect. If you find yourself in an involuntary disconnect experience, just go to the light.

> Yes. If faced with an involuntary disconnect experience, move forward toward the light and embrace what you see or experience. Do not be afraid. You will see the truth about Lyra and have

the opportunity to make the journey to the World of Immortality.

Before we end this discussion, we'd like to ask if there have been any correct disseminations of the Perseus myth?

> There is a sculpture that was an attempt to disseminate a correct understanding of the Medusa mythology. Please refer to the artist known as Benvenuto Cellini. This Being has constructed a Perseus statue that is currently located in the geographic region of Florence, Italy.

NOTE: Benvenuto Cellini was an Italian artist in 16th century AD. The statue known as "Perseus with the Head of Medusa" was erected in 1554 in Florence and commissioned by Duke Cosimo de'Medici I. The sculpture is made entirely of bronze and depicts Perseus raising Medusa's severed head. It is currently standing in the Loggia dei Lanzi of the Piazza della Signoria.

What is the correct understanding that Benvenuto Cellini was disseminating with this artwork?

> The holding of the head and the slaying of the Gorgon or Medusa exemplifies that the godhead is within your grasp.

Please elaborate on what you mean by the term "godhead".

> Please understand that light is equivalent to awareness. Your awareness grows exponentially as you absorb the light. The fact that you generate ideas in your head is the symbolism that is depicted by Perseus holding the Medusa head. You create the

> beliefs and you create the awareness. If you would like a basic description: You are responsible for turning this back on. The ability to reconnect is your own. The ability to be a transmitter and a transmitter of light is also your own innate ability and what you would call your birthright. The holding up of Medusa's head – as a trophy – is a call for you all to reassume this ability.

Medusa's face is not definitively female in Cellini's sculpture. It looks as masculine as the face on Perseus.

> This is the severing of the understanding that the godhead is a male attribute.

What is the more appropriate understanding?

> The origin of the light and your existence is best understood in a goddess head form. The cords of light that are originating from The Channel are also cords or channels of light that you will be forming and creating as you further your dissemination. The serpents on Medusa's head are equated with the cords of light, as we have already explained.

This is how the Medusa myth has steered us away from ourselves – by vilifying the Medusa, which resembles The Channel.

> Yes. You have created a myth around the slaying of a seemingly monstrous apparition that is in fact your origin. It is of the greatest importance that you continue to redefine this myth. The tale of Perseus is telling you about your ascension and the reality in your trapped state in the Earth plane density.

5

The Nimbus

Are there other depictions of The Channel in our histories and stories?

> The Aten, the Eucharist and Medusa are all a resemblance of the same entity we are calling The Channel. We would now like to direct you to a complete discussion about the nimbus.

NOTE: The nimbus is a solid disk of light, painted around or over the head of a sacred personage or prominent figure in art. It is similar to a halo.

What can you tell us about the nimbus?

> The "saintly" or "sacred" figures that are depicted or painted with a nimbus do not represent or signify that there is a "moral" way to exist. The understanding that the nimbus represents the light and The Channel is a correct understanding.

We've mistaken the Source of our existence for a heavenly hat. Is that what you're suggesting?

> The Channel is represented in all the symbols that are indicating a connection with a "Higher" or "Holy Spirit". The nimbus term has also come to define the clouds in your atmosphere and there is specific reason for this.

NOTE: A nimbus is also a "rain cloud".

Are you referring to the definition of nimbus, as in a cloud?

> These symbols for The Channel are veiled or "clouded" references to the Source of your

> existence. Your Bible books contain many descriptions of "clouds" that have been ignored and misunderstood.

Please cite an example of this.

> In the Bible book known as Revelation there is a passage prophesying the return of the Jesus Being. Please examine the mention of a cloud.

NOTE: The cited passage is found in the New Testament Book of Revelation chapter 1, verse 7.

"Behold, he cometh with clouds, and every eye shall see him: and all kindreds of the Earth shall wail because of him."

What was the original text?

> "Behold, cometh The Light, and every eye shall see it: and all kindreds of the Earth shall unite and become it."

The original text establishes that we are all adjoined to the Light. The hijacked version simply inserts Jesus to subjugate us to a Ruler.

> This is a correct assessment.

To quickly review, the nimbus disc and the cloud are both representing The Channel – in artwork and Scripture. Is this is a correct understanding?

> This is correct.

Did artists use and apply the nimbus as a secret code – to indicate who was of Sirius origin?

> Sirius Beings applied the nimbus through works of art as a means to disseminate and circulate information. The truth about the nimbus is that there was a conscription movement to gather those Beings who had awareness of the connection with Sirius. The initial use of a nimbus or halo in artwork was to designate those Beings who are in alignment and were on a quest to disseminate and not misappropriate information.

Rulers and political figures were also painted with the nimbus.

> A hijacking of the use was initiated to further create confusion and then this ultimately led to an artistic fashion of the day.

From what linear date onward was it hijacked?

> Prior to 663 AD there was a very important intention to the application of the nimbus and halo.

Is there anything more you'd like to add to this discussion?

> There is an understanding that the Sirius Beings that have been left behind have continued to disseminate information in allegories. The nimbus, the Aten, the Eucharist and the Medusa Being are all examples of how you continue to remain trapped by your own allegories and religious treatises.

Wasn't the use of allegory also a way to thwart the authorities?

> This is not a question of the use of allegory. This is a question of impact. Most of your mythologies and stories that are available for public consumption are too easily hijacked. They have almost all been modified and are containing instructions to continue an existence that is split from the origin of your existence.

Are you using the word "split" in a specific context or simply saying that we lost contact with our Source?

> The split is represented in many ways, the most apparent one being reflected in your male/female paradigm. **In actuality, there is no gender split or any split in the assembly of light. Your belief in a split is what has created the Earth plane experience.**

Why would the thought of splitting off even enter the consciousness of a Light Being?

> This will be addressed in a subsequent Volume, as it is an advanced discussion and requires further understanding of the principles in your Volume 2 dissemination.

You previously suggested that The Channel can be "equated with a female aspect". Now you're saying there is no gender split in the assembly of light.

> This correlation with a female aspect was suggested in order for you to better understand the connection

that this Being has to your existence. In actuality there is no inherent gender split in The Channel.

Please elaborate.

What will help is a correction of your understanding of the Garden of Eden story. This will reveal another representation of The Channel.

What exactly are we correcting about the Garden of Eden story?

You will be correcting the belief that you have come from Fallen Angels or angels of fallen experience. This is not a correct understanding. The understanding that you all have the ability to return to the Tree that you originate from will also be corrected.

The Tree?

We will be discussing your Tree of Life allegory.

Is there anything more that we need to understand about the nimbus?

The disconnect experience is a unified experience. The understanding that some Beings can be regarded as in light or free of form or "saintly" is not a precise understanding.

Do you mean that Saints or elevated Beings do not exist?

You are all "Saints", as in you all originate in light. The depiction of the nimbus was not meant to elevate specific Beings. It was intended to steer you toward each other and to the Source of your existence. You will not see a Being with a nimbus or halo. When you are in light, you are all in light.

6

The Garden of Eden

The Tree of Life is a widespread archetype and religious symbol. Nearly all major religions and mythologies make use of it. We'd like to discuss this symbolism.

NOTE: The Tree of Life or Cosmic Tree is a common motif in religion and mythology that helps to explain the interconnectedness between Heaven and Earth.

> The Tree of Life is not a physical tree. This is actually representing The Channel. What you must understand is that The Channel represents the template for the change. When the Sirius group reassembles and returns home then the understanding of the Tree of Life will once again be spoken about.

You're saying that the Tree of Life symbolism found in a multitude of religions and belief systems is an attempt to describe The Channel. Is that correct?

> The appearance of The Channel and the cords of light have been interpreted, in this allegory, as the towering Tree and its branches. This is what you will redefine in your dissemination.

Can you explain again why this Being, The Channel, exists in the tunnel experience?

> In order to allow for travel through the gateway or the gateway of knowledge, this must be a "doorway" that is kept open. There is a fundamental starting point that is explained in the Book of Genesis.

Are we all becoming this Tree?

You will all meet at this Tree or in other words, The Channel. This is the Ascension Event.

We would like to achieve a new understanding of the Garden of Eden story in the Book of Genesis.

NOTE: The Garden of Eden story is found in the Bible book of Genesis – Old Testament. Adam and Eve, the first man and woman are created by God and allowed to inhabit the Earthly Paradise of Eden. God tells Adam that he can eat from all the trees in the garden except for one – the Tree of the Knowledge of Good and Evil. A serpent persuades Eve to eat from the forbidden Tree and this decision leads to their fall and expulsion from Eden.

What have we misinterpreted from this story?

> The Garden of Eden in this story is not a paradise. It is the obstruction.

Please elaborate.

> The actual "fall" from Eden is the Repair Project that you are involved in. Beings from your group have fallen from the true Eden to rescue you from your 3rd density Earth plane experience. The understanding that you have been thrown out of the Garden for disobedience is incorrect. Adam and Eve's existence in the Garden is the beginning of your fall. The Garden depicted in Genesis is not a paradise. It is your Earthly prison.

This is the complete opposite of what religions teach.

> The Garden of Eden in this parable represents the obstruction. This is the beginning of your misunderstanding. The Garden of Eden of this parable is not a paradise. It is representational of your obstructed existence.

What was the intention of the Garden of Eden parable?

> The Bible and specifically the Garden of Eden is actually a message for aid or assistance. It is not a beautiful allegory and moral treatise that will help you re-establish yourself in the "Kingdom of God". The understanding that there was a fall is correct in that there is help and assistance required.

Are you saying that the author wrote this parable as a distress signal?

> This parable is equivalent to a note asking for help or an urgent plea for emergency assistance. This has been staring at you all in the face for many millennia. The correction is being made now and the rescue mission and repair will culminate during the 2034-2060 linear time period.

If this is true then what will happen to the Bible or religion once the Sirius Beings are rescued or ascend en masse?

> The Bible will no longer be needed. There will be an implosion of religion and a reformation of the idea of religion. Those Beings affiliated with the Bible – the Sirius Beings – will be ascending and those Beings who remain in the Earth plane existence will remain and continue to be confused.

Will they ever be rescued?

> Yes. There will be a rescue and Repair Mission that is suitable for this group of Beings. Your undertaking will also help those who are remaining behind, as they will have questions about how they are aligned with the Bible. There will be outrage and a multitude of questions about the many reformations of religious ideals over the centuries. They will come to understand that these reformations and corrections resulted in the diminishment of the light.

Are you saying that the Abrahamic based bible stories were written for Sirius Beings?

> The Bible specifically refers to the Beings that are linked to the Sirius experience. The Bible is not a manuscript or an allegory that is accessible for all. It has been borrowed and manipulated. The original message was clear: there are trapped Beings who require the assistance in the homeward journey.

Will the Beings that are left behind after the 2034 Ascension Event understand what has occurred?

> There will be a dramatic change in the weather pattern and systems in the Earth plane density. You are currently referring to this as "climate change" and "global warming". The mass ascension event will trigger more of this experience and be attributed to "climate change".

NOTE: Global warming refers to the gradual increase in the average temperature world wide due to the burning of fossil fuels like oil, coal and natural gas. Deforestation and soil erosion also contribute to the anthropogenic carbon dioxide emissions.

What else will occur after the mass Ascension Event?

> The luminaries will change position. The understanding that the luminaries are shifting will be evident and not hidden when the mass ascension experience occurs.

We'd like to return to the parable. In Genesis chapter 2, verse 17 why does God say the following to Adam: "But of the Tree of the Knowledge of Good and Evil you shall not eat, for the day that you eat of it you shall surely die"

> If you subscribe to your correct origin and wish to make the disconnect experience you will not "surely die" if this is a voluntary disconnect.

What if it is an involuntary disconnect experience?

> There is still an opportunity to ascend via the "death experience" if you are properly informed and prepared. Please encourage your readership to choose the voluntary disconnect experience, for this is the path of certainty.

Can we conclude that what God tells Adam of the forbidden fruit is a complete lie?

> This is simply a complete lie and misrepresentation. This is to turn Beings away from the Source of their existence and the light. The death experience is something that is feared and the disconnect

experience has now been taught as the end of your existence when in fact it is an opportunity for change and ascension.

Death is not the end. It is an opportunity to return to a freeform existence.

There is always an opportunity for change and ascension whether you voluntarily disconnect or suffer an involuntary disconnect.

What more can you tell us about the Tree of Life allegory as it pertains to The Channel?

The origin of the Tree and the origin of your existence are confirmed by a split, a split in your existence and a split in your comprehension and understanding.

Are you saying that our confusion about an afterlife is confirmation that there is an "afterlife"?

This is a correct understanding. The split is what you need to confirm with your readers. We are speaking about the split in the understanding that there has always been a singular path to reconnect with the homeward journey.

That singular path is The Channel – is that correct?

Yes and The Channel and its channels of light and cords of ascension is represented by the Tree. The Channel is a singular experience and has been trapped as the knowledge has been taken away from you. You no longer remember as your gateway of knowledge is blocked. You are now remembering the Source of the light and the Source of the existence.

There are two Trees mentioned in the parable of the Garden of Eden – the Tree of Knowledge of Good and Evil and the Tree of Life. Is this another representation of the split?

> Yes. The original tale of the Garden of Eden was disseminated with a two-tree account. This was to help you understand how the truth was corrupted and how you can reconstruct your belief stream. This was a parable to help you re-embrace your origin. Your origin experience, in this allegory, was attributed to a Tree or a Tree-like existence.

Are you saying that we are re-joining the Tree or The Channel?

> This is a precise understanding.

We'd also like for you to clarify the meaning behind Eve's actions in this parable. She follows the guidance of the serpent and eats the "forbidden fruit".

> What you are witnessing in this account is an acknowledgement that when you believe in the light you will fall away from the beliefs that are holding you in form. Eve is connecting to the light-form existence.

We do however contain light during time travel.

> There is a temporary containment of light in order to move the light but containing light must never

occur, as light is meant to be free, as you are all existing naturally.

Eve eating the apple is representative of her connection with The Channel or the Source. Is that an accurate understanding?

> The Being who consumes the apple is partaking in the truthful experience. Eve is remaining connected with the source of the nourishment, as is being explained in the allegory. She is not passive or unintelligent or naive by heeding the serpent's advice. This misconception must be corrected.

Has this been an attempt to steer us away from energy of the divine feminine?

> This is one example, yes. Eve is connecting with the light without resistance and partaking and celebrating in the light. The misunderstanding that all evil is connected with "Eve's mistake" needs to be corrected. This is an advanced discussion in this place and space and must be introduced in layers.

This would mean that Adam represents the misguided Being, as he is hesitant to eat the apple.

> You have Beings who are knowledgeable and aware (Eve) and you have Beings that are not (Adam). You have created an existence in your present linear timeframe where there are females who are deemed passive and receptive. They are in fact connected, albeit mostly unconsciously. The male gender experience is taking action and trying to repair but is mostly disconnected form the Source. You are all

trapped and must redirect your awareness toward the light.

While men are largely accountable for perpetuating harmful power structures, women in today's society have to a significant degree enslaved themselves to consumerism. How are women in this instance "connected" as you put it?

> The female energy can accept the light and the truth of their origin willingly. The question is how do you modify the consumptive and materialistic patterns that are preoccupying your existence. Women have become increasingly entrapped by consumerism. There is a movement on the horizon however. Women are choosing to re-modify their beliefs and will start to speak out about the broader changes that must occur in the Earth plane existence.

Are you speaking about the 3rd wave feminist movement that is occurring mostly in the USA?

> This on the surface looks like women's rights and the voice for "feminism". Their outspokenness however is an unconscious release of the light.

Individuals who wish to create a "gender war" have hijacked the current Feminist movement. You're saying that this is an unconscious movement to release the light – is that correct?

> Yes. There is an energy and momentum that is being created to release yourselves from the male/female gender split. The problem is that this movement to hand over "the power" to female Beings is the derailment of the true intention. The power to run a civilization should not be the goal.

What should the goal be?

> It should be to release yourselves from your incorrect belief streams. Females and males should all want the "power" to escape your form through the voluntary disconnect experience. You must all re-embrace your connection with the light and no longer believe that light exists in different forms.

We must all return to the Tree – or The Channel.

> The Channel is the access for all of you. In the analogy or symbolism of the Tree and the Tree of Life, this is the access. The branches of the Tree represent the cords of light. The branches or the cords of light are available for you all. We are bringing you back to this existence and understanding. Beings of Sirius are making their final journey homeward.

7

Michelangelo's Lost Statue

We've spoken about some literary and artistic representations of The Channel. Can we also involve the Reader in a new discovery – perhaps suggest an excursion readers can take to view some evidence?

> You will be revealing a discovery in a subsequent Volume. Your readers will need to be prepared for this information.

Where will the discovery occur?

> There is a specific fountain in the geographic location of Rome, Italy. The fountain contains truths and a written treatment that is disguised as an allegory. Your readers will inevitably ask "what fountain and who is the sculptor?" You will reveal this information once you have both undertaken the mission.

Is the message or inscription presented on a plaque?

> The text is located on the side of the fountain. It is not inscribed onto a plaque. It is hidden and in order to see it you must know what you are looking for. This is a complicated experience that you will map out for your readership in a subsequent Volume.

What is the allegory or message that is inscribed?

> It is a short paragraph of text that contains a rhyme and a seemingly playful verse. This could not be any further from the truth. This fountain and sculpture are an example of a great effort to contain a

permanent and important message in stone. Nobody is paying any attention to it.

Is the verse written in Latin or Italian and can we translate it for our readers?

> You are not dealing with Latin, Greek, English, Italian or any ancient language. You are dealing with symbols that you are not well versed in and there must be no error in the transmission of information. The inscription states that there is light that reawakens those that seek it. The few Beings who have read the inscription are not aware of the origin of it. They believe that it is a religious or a biblical context. This is incorrect.

Can the inscription be captured in a photograph?

> The photographs will show a contrast as in light and dark areas. There is an inscription that must be felt with your hand and not seen with your eyes. There is an assembly of fountains that is done in a way where pieces create an intersection and a letter or a symbol. There are symbols in these fountains. You are beginning with one particular fountain. If you are to feel with your hands you will understand there is an inscription that must be disseminated.

We'd like to publish the instruction for the readers so that they can also take the journey and see for themselves.

> You will have more instruction and information. This information is not specifically disseminated in Volume 2, as you are now discovering the purpose of the undertaking. The Perseus statue and the

holding of the head resemble something that you will also find in the fountain structure. You must make a correlation between the importance of this fountain and what the Statue of Perseus represents.

Is there any other part of the fountain that we should inspect?

This fountain is containing parts of a figure or statue that do not belong there. There is a fight about the pieces that assemble the fountain and the message in the text is ignored. The reason for the addition of the text is an initiative to disseminate information and this has been overlooked completely. There are also mineral deposits, which make it difficult to decipher what you are looking at. The reason for the leaching and the mineral deposits – that need to be repeatedly removed – is that the construction of the fountain did not occur in a singular plan.

Please elaborate.

There are pieces on this fountain that belong to a separate statue. These pieces are arms that have been attached to the fountain in a way that you do not recognize their origin. The arms or appendages have a connection to a work from Michelangelo.

Is this a lost statue of Michelangelo's?

There are sculptures and artwork that have been used to disseminate truths and subsequently destroyed. The reassembly of some of Michelangelo's artwork is such that the original message is no longer contained in the original impression or model of the statue. There are codes

> and very specific messages that are contained in this Being's artwork that have been effectively demolished and destroyed by virtue of reassembling his works in other structures.

Why were these artworks left in pieces and not destroyed in their entirety?

> The individuals who were responsible with the task of destroying and removing the artwork chose to hide pieces. This was done so that a message could be relayed to the public awareness in the "future". The difficulty is that this statue is now found in many different places within a specific area of Rome.

Who or what was the statue depicting?

> This statue is a recreation of the encounter with The Channel in the involuntary disconnect journey. The decision that one makes to continue the ascension and immortal state instead of recycling back into the reincarnation experience was expressed in this sculpture. The piece was misunderstood but was seen as controversial for a different reason.

What was the main reason for the controversy?

> It depicted a female in a responsibility and role that would imply that the female made the decision for the universe and the world of beyond. The understanding that the god was depicted in a goddess form is what was adversarial. This was not a comfortable alliance with the ideas of the day.

Did the statue depict a traditional god with female traits?

> The statue was a hermaphroditic image and this image is close to what you know as Priapus.

NOTE: Priapus was a Greek fertility god often depicted with a large erect phallus. He was regarded as the protector of gardens and was the offspring of Aphrodite and Dionysus.

Priapus was the god of fertility. What does his function have to do with "the world of beyond"?

> You must reorganize your beliefs about fertility and about what the god and goddess of fertility represent. The original statue is representative of the continuing reassembly of the Light Body and reconnection with the voluntary disconnect. The awareness of this process is told in a story about fertility as in self-fertility – as in the Ouroboros construct.

NOTE: The Ouroboros is an ancient symbol of a serpent eating its own tail. It is believed to symbolize infinity or the cycle of birth and death.

To clarify, Michelangelo sculpted a statue of Priapus but depicted the god with female traits. Is that correct?

> The sculpture was a hermaphroditic image of the Priapus Being but also containing the channels or the snakes as you are referring to them from the Medusa image. This sculpture is a combination of what you are referring to as the Gorgon and also a very masculine image. This is originally a bi-sexual image in that this was not a female or male energy.

This statue challenged the traditional notion of a Father God.

> This is correct but more importantly it told the story of the origin of your Light – The Channel. There is a hidden truth about the light and the light coming out through the channels. These channels are also depicted in Genesis as the rivers and in the snakes from Medusa's head.

The channels of light are depicted as the rivers in Genesis. Should we also look for references to bodies of water elsewhere in our mythologies?

> What you must inform your readers about is that there is a specific reason for the symbolism of fountain structure.

What are fountains symbolizing?

> Fountains are a complete representation of your ideas about The Channel or Source of your Light. This is the reason why many of you are "enchanted" by the fountain structure.

Are you suggesting that fountains were originally designed to represent The Channel?

> This is correct. Michelangelo's lost statue was also directing you all to the Source of your light.

Are there any depictions of or references to this statue in existence today?

> Michelangelo's drawings and plans of this statue are held in the building you refer to as the Pitti Palace in Florence, Italy.

Please explain further what Priapus symbolizes and why Michelangelo chose to depict him in this manner.

> Priapus was originally considered to be a messenger god. The Romans however, idealized what they thought was tantamount to the building of their Empire. The understanding that Priapus has a function that is more aligned with Mercury and Hermes will not be received in a positive or acceptable light, as the understanding does not align with the current and present misconception.

NOTE: In the Greek pantheon of gods, Hermes is primarily the deity of herald and trade. He is the son of Zeus and a nymph named Maia. Immediately after his birth he stole Apollo's herd of cattle and invented the lyre instrument from a tortoise shell. During the Hellenistic period, Hermes was conflated with the Egyptian god of wisdom, Thoth. Mercury is his Roman counterpart.

What is the current misconception?

> The misconception is that Priapus represents the source of the food and the nourishment of the Earth. This is an incorrect belief. The source and the nourishment for the light is what you need to explain. Priapus in the correct understanding is the

utilization of the light and the light source, which is something that Man Being has forgotten.

Priapus was turned into a symbol of fertility, reproduction, food and nourishment. In actuality he was a Messenger of light. Is that correct?

> If you consider The Channel as the Tree and if you consider Priapus as the access and absorption of the light then you will further understand that in order to become "part of this Tree" you must utilize the proper parameters. These parameters are not intellectual. They are absorbed light codes.

Readers might be confused by your use of the term "code".

> Please understand that a code is a belief stream. You are absorbing new codes as in belief streams. Light awareness does not require a mathematic formula or quantum physics understanding. This is simply akin to Man Being taking a drink of water.

How do we absorb a belief stream through a symbol or deity e.g. Priapus?

> Priapus is an understanding that you are not fertilized or nourished from Being to Being. You are nourished through the light. Accepting this belief stream is like drinking water. There is absorption.

When you say "nourished from Being to Being" are you speaking about procreation?

> This is correct. You are all seeking the correction of your DNA through the experience of reproducing

yourselves. You believe this is a means from which you can achieve the voluntary disconnect and release of the Light Being to Lyra. This is an incorrect belief stream. We will continue this topic in another discussion. For now you will need to address the role of the Vatican Group as this dialogue will stir many questions concerning the seemingly contradictory nature of this Organization.

What is the Vatican's ultimate agenda?

They are involved in ensuring the deficiency in the luminosity. As the deprivation of light continues, the need for religion is sustained. The need for religion is a replacement for the light.

The church commissioned Michelangelo for several works. Why does the Vatican – today – risk their agenda by leaving such subversive artwork in plain sight of the public?

There was a Pope who made a new decision and that decision was to embrace the light and abandon the values that were being instilled in the Christian belief system. The Pope in question had an encounter with Lyra and had ascension experience.

What was this Pope's name?

Pope Gregor XIII. The undertaking to disseminate was clearly not available to him because of the nature of his Office. His position would make it impossible to attempt to relay a new understanding.

Did Pope Gregor XIII allow these coded works of art to be exhibited?

> Yes. This was an attempt to disseminate by reinstating the information in the artwork in Rome. He placed them where visitors can walk freely and visit the pieces – and hopefully absorb the information.

Does the Vatican currently have knowledge of the particular fountain inscription and what it means?

> They do not have complete awareness. There is another group with full knowledge about the message.

What group are you referring to?

> The knowledge is passed amongst those who follow a cloistered sect of Christianity.

What exactly do you mean by "sect of Christianity"?

> We are suggesting to you that there is another path of Christianity that is being practiced and followed and not widely known about.

What is the name of this sect?

> The name is Aegis Order of the Battista.

When was this sect created?

> This was an organization that was created around the time of 65 AD. This was a decision to contain the knowledge and pursue the hidden mysteries in an underground vehicle. This is a group of Beings

that arrived in Basilicata (Italy) from a region close to the Euphrates.

What is the origin of their teachings if not traditional Christianity?

> This group is specifically aligned with the experience that occurred with the Jesus Being. The original sect was assembled from the followers of the Being you are calling Peter, as in the "disciple" of Jesus Christ.

Peter's disciples started this Order. Is that correct?

> This is a correct understanding. The responsible dissemination and activity of this sect stems today from the region of Basilicata in Italy. This group remains true to the origin and has not shifted the belief or the teachings in any way that would allow for a new understanding or recreation.

When you say that this group remains "true to the origin" are you saying that they are preserving and administering Jesus' true teachings?

> This is correct if you accept and believe that Jesus was disseminating the understanding of Lyra and the Lemuria state. Today the Aegis Order of Battista is subscribing to this original sect and continues to practice in secret. Their religious affiliation to the world is somewhat different to what they follow.

Is the Vatican aware of the Aegis Order of the Battista?

> As unbelievable as it may seem to you all, the Vatican is not completely aware of this, as there are Heads of State as well as Heads of Organizations who are involved in this underground sect. It is therefore once again hidden in plain sight.

The general population is fed lies and kept busy by a privileged class that is in full possession of ascension knowledge.

> It is a most unfortunate paradigm. This is affiliated specifically with your questions about how Rulers and individuals of status were and are equipped with the understanding of the shape shifting capability.

How many individuals are following the teachings of this specific sect of Christianity?

> The movement of this sect had reached an untenable number in the 1600s and remains today a vast network of Beings worldwide. This Order exists today because of the infrastructure allotted to them by those Beings with power, influence and status. For this reason especially it is being kept from the "common person".

The Reader will want to know who exactly these Heads of State are.

> There is nothing to gain with that specific knowledge. Your readers can be assured with the knowledge that "power" will soon shift toward the Light. As you all begin to shift your beliefs the network of lies will inevitably collapse. This is why

you have all been "kept in the dark". Shift your beliefs and you shift the paradigm.

Is there anything more that the Reader needs to know about Aegis Order of the Battista?

> They had and have the true knowledge of the rite of Baptism.

What is the true knowledge of Baptism?

> Witnessing the voluntary disconnect.

Please elaborate.

> Please believe that there are witnesses to this experience of the voluntary disconnect. The Baptismal rite is defined by the assistance in the voluntary disconnect experience.

How does one assist in this experience?

> The assistance is a guidance that is offered to those who have absorbed the knowledge and to those who teach the knowledge. The voluntary disconnect decision is a singular and independent rite of decision and commitment.

This completely contradicts the Baptism of infants who have the "rite" forced onto them.

> The Baptismal rites have now been perverted and misunderstood as an initiation into the initial stages of a religious path. In actuality, baptism is an

initiation for the final stages of your existence in the physical Earth form.

"True Baptism" refers to the administering of ascension knowledge. The Baptismal rite is not a dipping of the head into water but a relaying of teachings in preparation for the disconnect experience. Is this correct?

> This is correct. There are keys that you can be handed if you have not traversed and made the reconnective state. There is an understanding and an explanation about the reconnective state of awareness in the Intermediary World of Lyra. This leads to the understanding of what you are referring to as the "Elysian Fields" state and Plant World consciousness.

NOTE: Ancient Greek and Roman poets Hesiod, Homer and Virgil all wrote of the Elysian Fields as an afterlife for the righteous.

Will we be discussing the Elysian Fields and Plant World Consciousness?

> Yes. This dialogue will be disseminated in Volume 2. These keys are contained in this dissemination and those readers who are undertaking this journey and experience will absorb the understanding. Those who are not ready to embrace the beliefs in the voluntary disconnect will not notice or experience the keys that are contained in Volume 2.

Is there any proof of the existence of this secret sect of Christianity?

Your readers will want to visit the "church" known as San Nicola di Bari in the geographic location of Bari, Italy.

NOTE: San Nicola di Bari was built in 1089 AD to house Saint Nicholas' skeletal remains. They were brought over from Myra, a city on the southern Mediterranean Seacoast (present day Turkey). The church is a popular pilgrimage site for devotees of the Catholic and Eastern Orthodox religions.

Two stone bulls – with horns removed – adorn either side of the exterior entrance to San Nicola di Bari. Why is that? Bulls are a pagan symbol.

> The original members of this church were involved with the secret sect we are discussing.

There are additional stone sculptures of creatures on either side of the interior entrance to the church. What are these sculptures depicting?

> This is the transformative state as these "creatures" are in between form. This is the shape shifting experience. The benefits of visiting the locations that we are discussing will soon avail themselves to you all.

Will the confirmation that we have been systematically kept in the dark deflate the Reader?

> What there is a lack of is more than compensated for in your new understanding – through this dissemination. You are reminding Man Being and your Soul Ascension Group Assembly that the source of their unfortunate existence is not about

money or geographical location or status or consumption. This is about rejoining in the design of your origin so that there can be a release to the homeward existence.

We are finally returning home.

The instantaneous release homeward will occur with the next opportunity and the Messianic release experience.

8

Procreation

MAN BEING

You said that the Romans idealized what they thought was important about Priapus. Are you referring to fertility, sex and sexuality?

> This is correct.

You've also mentioned that we are seeking the correction of our DNA through reproduction and that this is an incorrect belief stream. Please elaborate.

> The belief that children hold the tomorrow is somewhat correct in that there is an undertaking to improve the DNA by learning to absorb more of the light. The understanding that you are consumers of knowledge is also correct and the understanding that Man Being is trying to create a more perfect Man Being is also correct. The drive to procreate is a drive for knowledge and perfection of the DNA. Ultimately this has failed and the continued compulsion to procreate is something that you are not consciously in control of.

Is our biological compulsion to reproduce and maintain the species an unconscious effort to correct our DNA?

> Yes. Man Being does not however need to procreate in order to perfect the DNA. The need to produce other Man Beings is not necessary if you equate the ascension experience as a reconnection of the Beings who belong in your Soul Ascension Group.

Are our offspring a part of our Soul Ascension Group?

> Those "Beings" that you are creating through procreation ultimately belong in your Soul

Ascension Group. An important distinction to make however is that creating a Being does not make more Beings. Creating a Being simply divides the energies and complicates the matter further.

Please elaborate.

This is not an answer that will be readily accepted but by creating and procreating you are not driving the ascension experience forward. There is a belief that souls are trapped and need a physical body to reincarnate into. This belief needs to be corrected.

What is the correct belief?

"Souls" who are not in a physical form in the Earth plane density are waiting in Lyra. They will be able to reunite with you when your soul ascension experience occurs. You do not "need" a physical body to continue existing.

Does this mean that by procreating we are holding our Soul Ascension Group back?

Beings in your Soul Ascension Group who are existing in the Earth plane will continue having children and procreating but there will be a lesser drive to do so. It is somewhat correct that there has been an irresponsible level of procreation in the world but this does not necessarily decrease your chances of ascension. It simply creates more confusion in that there are now seemingly more Beings that need to be rescued.

Our offspring are just a splitting off from our Light Being and not a separate Being. Is that correct?

> What we would like to define with you in this dialogue is that procreating does not necessarily equate to the addition of a Human Being. When there is a procreation event the light and the light codes have been somewhat diminished and divided.

This might be a challenging concept to absorb.

> Yes. There are more Beings on Earth than are really in existence. The understanding that you are splitting and dividing your energy and light is a revelation. The divisions of the light and your awareness have included many events of procreation and many Beings have been "created" from your original Being. You are not creating a new Light Being. You are dividing an already existing one.

There are also Beings or entities that we call "ghosts". These Beings appear to inhabit the Earth plane without experiencing a procreation event or reincarnation. How is that occurring?

> These discarnate entities are Beings who are somewhat trapped in that there is no form for them to enter.

Why are they trapped in this way?

> Their beliefs are strong enough to make the commitment to stay out of physical form but not strong enough to rebuild their Light Body. Your purported connection with the "spirit world"

continues as a result. These are Beings who are remaining in a "limbo" experience.

What are these discarnate Beings seeking by entering the 3rd density Earth plane?

> As you shift your beliefs in the 3rd density, you are concurrently building your Light Body in Lyra. The discarnate experience is similar to your Light Body. The difference is that you do not have your physical Being or body in the Earth plane to communicate with. The discarnate Beings, or "ghosts" as you refer to them, are turning to others in the Earth density for assistance.

Are you saying that these Beings are lacking the necessary information to achieve the full Light Body release and need us to provide it?

> This is correct. They are essentially waiting for others to provide the ascension event. They are "Waiters", in essence. The mission of the Repair Project is not only to reformat your beliefs but to also help others.

We'd like to return to the procreation event. Please explain the process by which a Being reincarnates and enters a female womb?

> First, a Being who "dies" with little or no awareness is making a choice to reenter a stream whereby the light defines them. This Being will not only see light around itself, but within itself. This confuses many of you and so you experience a belief that you must be contained in a physical body form in order to

exist. This belief creates a form and this creation of form is the procreation event.

Who is controlling the procreation – the Earth couple or the Being who is experiencing the involuntary disconnect?

> The Being who is making the involuntary disconnect experience is controlling the procreation event. Your belief to exist in form connects with the signals from the 3rd density Earth plane "couple". The beliefs are connected.

As soon as the Being decides to exist in form, a procreation event occurs with an Earth couple that similarly desires to "create a human form". Is that correct?

> Simplified, but yes. The belief that to "be existing" means to be "in form" is creating the cycle of procreation and reincarnation. Procreation and reincarnation are equal.

This requires a monumental shift in belief.

> This is a concept that is not understood and the idea of procreation only weakened the chance for ascension, as you are further divided.

Have we damaged our DNA by procreating and dividing the light?

> You are creating and have created offshoots of yourself. The point that we are explaining with you is that you must understand the Source of your light to remain connected to it. The understanding that dividing the light and procreating to create more

Beings in a quest for information is not the source of your problem. It is the ramification of the system and the authority that led you to this place and space in your existence.

What are you referring to when you say an "authority led us" to this problem?

Please refer to the Being you know as Caligula.

NOTE: Caligula was the 3rd Emperor of Rome and reigned from 37-41 AD. He succeeded Tiberius and is described as having been a noble and moderate Ruler for a short period before repositioning himself as a sex crazed, sadistic, perverted tyrant.

What can you tell us about Caligula?

Caligula made it a mission to destroy others as in soul destruction and soul ascension destruction.

How specifically did he do that?

This was achieved by encouraging the act of procreation and sexual activity. This encouraged the diminishment of the DNA and the light awareness.

Caligula's sexual perversions led us astray.

The physicality of the events that have occurred in Caligula's lifetime encouraged Man Being to remain in the physical form. Man Being began seeking contentment and pleasure in the physical form in a way that had not been previously practiced.

> Focusing your existence on the enjoyment of physical pleasure does not assist in your ascension.

Caligula's sexual exploits and perversions had a knock-on effect with the populace. Is that what you're saying?

> Yes. The idea that being in the physical form can create the utmost amount of pleasure is an incorrect belief system. This belief system was instated during Caligula's reign and adventures. The monumental deficiency was created during this linear time period in that the events of the physical experience became more and more enjoyable and more highly regarded as the utmost in existence.

Is our desire for sexual pleasure that prevalent in our lives?

> The sexual act and procreation is driving all of the behaviour and the consumptive madness in the Earth plane density.

Caligula was regarded as a tyrant by his contemporaries and was ultimately assassinated. How could he have impacted people if he wasn't respected?

> The belief that he was not respected is one attitude but the influence that he created is another. There are activities that Man Being shuns away from on the surface – but wonders about privately.

He modeled another way to experience sex, albeit perverse, and created a curiosity and shift toward sexual pleasure and procreation. Is that accurate?

> Yes. The experiences that were written about Caligula in the time period caused a monumental shift in a new awareness of the physical form. The boundaries of enjoyment in the physical form were crossed in such a way that the physical form seemed to be immune from any damage by undertaking activity such as incest.

NOTE: Roman Historian Suetonius, who lived in the 1st century AD, wrote of Caligula: "He lived in the habit of incest with all his sisters; and at table, when much company was present, he placed each of them in turns below him".

This depraved behavior led to a shift in attitude toward sexuality and our physical nature – and inevitably to more procreation. Is this Caligula's legacy?

> This is accurate. Procreation does not create a form. Procreation creates a divide in the light and divide in the Light Being awareness.

What was Man Being's attitude toward procreation and sexuality before Caligula?

> Before the time period of the Jesus experience, procreation was enjoyed but the assembly of beliefs was such that there was a yearning to return homeward. The question about the ties and alliances in the Earth plane existence were also more carefully examined. This was a period where beliefs were closer to being aligned with the voluntary disconnect experience. There was respect for the Light Body assembly and the idea of existing in light was prevalent leading up to Jesus' dissemination and shortly afterward.

People were enjoying sex and procreating long before Caligula existed. It's difficult to understand how one misguided individual could have such an impact.

> The Caligula Being will be revisited in subsequent Volumes as this Being's energy is aligned with a destructive agenda. There is more to the "Caligula story" that your readers will learn about. Before this Being existed, procreation was an attempt to repair the DNA and was more consciously observed. After Jesus and the time period during Caligula there was an introduction of new ideas and beliefs. The enjoyment of the physical form and flesh became more important than repairing the DNA. The knowledge was soon lost as the literature and the attention turned to the physical form.

What role did religions play in our outlook on sex and procreation?

> Religious organizations tried to control the interest in physical pleasure merely because they feared it would topple people's need for religion and religious authority. In this effort religion created a further fervor by making sex taboo. Religious organizations mandating that you all behave and procreate under certain conditions only made this more interesting for Man Being.

NOTE: The Catechism of the Catholic Church states the following regarding chastity and sexuality: "Lust is disordered desire for or inordinate enjoyment of sexual pleasure. Sexual pleasure is morally disordered when sought for itself, isolated from its procreative and unitive purposes".

Why is the sexual orgasm so euphoric if it ultimately leads us away from the light?

> Orgasm as you are experiencing now in your physical form is equivalent to the experience of the voluntary disconnect. This is something that you are vaguely remembering as the experience that you all seek is the return homeward.

You just equated the orgasm with the voluntary disconnect. Please elaborate.

> The idea that you can have a physical connection with another Being in order to release the light is somewhat correct in that you are unconsciously attempting to repair the abhorrent DNA. The release of the light however is a permanent experience. The orgasm is not.

Why does the orgasm still feel so euphoric?

> There is still some remembrance that the DNA must be repaired and the Light Body must be rebuilt. There is also a remembrance that the Soul Ascension Group must be assembled through a voluntary disconnect experience. You are remembering something but understanding it incorrectly.

The orgasm is a reminder of ascension because it was experienced in order to repair our DNA. Is that correct?

> You have all equated the positive benefits of the orgasm to the enjoyment of the physical form. In actuality these sensations are an alignment of

energies or frequencies that occur in the voluntary disconnect experience. **You are all striving to voluntarily disconnect and this is what is driving you to seek pleasure in the flesh.**

Is this a recommendation to stop procreating?

> There is no recommendation to abstain from sex or stop procreating. There is nothing "wrong" with these events. What we are suggesting is that you can align this energy and experience and have the same sensations by being in Light.

Yet you are saying that procreation is diminishing the light.

> Procreation is no longer what it was intended to be. It was an attempt to reform the understanding and reassemble the DNA codes to fix the abhorrent places on the DNA code strand. We are not proposing that you must stop having sex but we are suggesting to you that the orgasm event that you are all seeking is just a pale shadow of the real experience and the event.

The real reason we enjoy sex is because it is intrinsically tied to our repair – but we have directed our focus onto the physical component of it.

> You are remembering an event that you have lost and equating the minor enjoyment that you are experiencing as a great achievement. It is the achievement of the orgasm that has misaligned your

thinking. This is not an achievement. This is a misinterpreted truth and an ineffectual experience.

9

Music

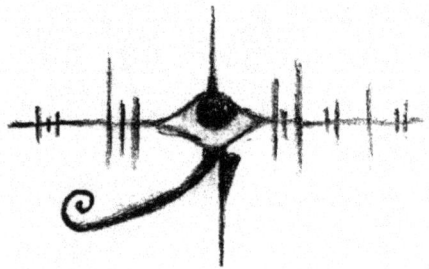

The orgasm experience represents our drive to achieve the voluntary disconnect. In its most elevated form, creating music can be similarly satisfying. What is the true function of music?

> There is much to understand about how the masses have been influenced in a positive way through this art form. This discussion will allow others to be more receptive to the information that is being disseminated in your books. The connection with the arts is what will welcome those who would previously not be interested in reading the dialogue.

Why is art a big point of interest?

> There are specific art forms that are attuned to the Sirius Beings and you will be uncovering these art forms as a way to represent the attempts to continue the Repair Project. These attempts and the cycle of creative bursts will continue. We will be explaining with you what the Sirius Beings have contributed in the arts.

How does each genre of music resonate with us?

> If you are directly asking us what music will benefit your ascension and development and process, we will speak on the different genres.

What can you tell us about Hip Hop and its popularity in North America?

> The reason for the increase in popularity is because the Information Age is aligned with the Hip-Hop genre. There are two types of artists operating in

this genre. The first are the Spoken Word artists whose intention is to disseminate information and codes through the music. The others are consciously choosing to disseminate confusion and contribute to the consumptive madness that is plaguing the Earth plane dimension.

Are you suggesting that the Internet Generation is attracted to the lyrical component of Hip-Hop – simply because of the volume of information packed into each song?

This is an accurate assessment. Hip-Hop can contribute to your ascension on the one hand but also contribute to a complete lack of awareness and attunement to awareness on the other. A simple adjustment can turn Hip Hop into a very powerful ascension tool.

Is there a musical movement or genre developing now that is precipitating the ascension event?

There is a systematic cultural shift and absorption of music that you are equating with past genres from other linear decades. Your "old music" is being modified with frequencies and sounds and beats through your "acid jazz" and "EDM" movements, for example.

NOTE: Acid Jazz is a musical genre that combines elements of jazz, funk and hip-hop. It developed in the UK during the 1980s/90s and could be interpreted as a fusion of Jazz/Funk and Dance/Pop. EDM stands for Electronic Dance Music, which is largely produced for festivals, clubs and raves. EDM is primarily composed of synth sounds and is defined through various sub genres such as House, Dubstep, Techno and Trance.

What are the components of "old music" that new artists are revisiting?

> There is much value in the older genre of music and composition as the intention when these pieces were created was to create a message that was readily absorbed. These messages still stand today in your linear time frame. Music can be seized as an opportunity to make people listen and be aware of the ability to listen. By listening we are referring to the feeling of the frequency and vibration. The need to be surrounded by music – whether or not one has the capacity to physically hear – is the reason why Man Being is able to make a monumental and very rapid shift toward ascension.

How does music facilitate such a "rapid shift"?

> Your cellular make-up allows for absorption of frequencies and signals that have profound and lasting effects. For this reason music must be chosen carefully. Music can be a potent form of subduing the masses and limiting the reconnective ability and reconnective patterning.

What type of music falls into this category?

> It is not difficult to ascertain which musicians and which musical genres are contributing to your consumptive and addictive patterns. You would be wise not to identify these musicians but rather inspire them to create music that is aligned with

ascension. These "popular" artists can contribute to ascension in monumental ways.

Is listening to popular music really derailing us from ascension?

> Listening to and absorbing the frequency of designed music is harmful much in the way that overeating is.

Are there modern musicians who are attuning to the frequencies that we are discussing in these Volumes?

> There is an engagement of the inner ear globally.

You're using the term "inner ear". Does that mean that the hearing impaired can still absorb music?

> For those who do not have the physical capacity to hear, there is a vibration and frequency that is still affecting your brain function. The physicality of listening to music will be changing en masse as artists are being encouraged to incorporate certain frequencies of sound and vibration in their music. This will also affect the ability to listen and receive and absorb code.

What are the specific frequencies that artists are being encouraged to incorporate into their music?

> There will be a key of D movement that composers will be consciously choosing to involve themselves with. This alignment will be a global function. Artists and composers and musicians will choose to collectively create and disseminate music in this key

at the same time – in order to shift and make a shift of the light.

NOTE: The key of D (D major) is a major scale based on D. Its key signature consists of two sharps – a sharp means higher pitch as opposed to a flat. The D major was regarded as "the Key of Glory" in the Baroque Period, as many trumpet concertos were in the Key of D.

Why is the key of D an effective tool for this shift?

> You have been made aware in Volume 1 that your Moon is being purposely regulated so that you are devoid of the proper amount of the absorption of light. The key of D at this place and space is aligned with the position of the Moon and the position of the luminosity. It is helping to realign you with the Moon and the luminosity.

Please explain how that occurs.

> The frequency obtained from specific keys can change the direction of light waves. Please be aware that the power of composition and song has more lasting resonance and benefit than you are presently aware. There will be a global attempt to shift the light waves and energy through the unison of sound waves. The sound waves are being produced through musical composition – collectively using a key choice, as in the key of D.

We are redirecting the light our way by composing music in the key of D.

> The frequencies emitted by the implementation of these musical keys allows for a lasting redirection of light waves. You are attempting to redirect the light so that there is maximum benefit for all. When Man Being is able to absorb light in the proper capacity there will be global awareness that there is a need to change.

What would our existence be without music?

> There is no sense in speaking this question, as there is no way to exist without the frequencies and vibrations you are speaking about. The ability for Man Being to exist requires an immersion in frequency and an expression of this frequency is easily absorbed through music.

Are you saying that sound is our stabilizer?

> The existing musical network and exchange of resonance and frequencies creates stabilization. This is what is preventing the commencement of a flood experience as in a sonic flood experience as in drowning in the sonic sea.

What defines the "sonic sea"?

> Frequencies and sounds and vibrations are released from your cellular phone networks and your machinery and appliances. These frequencies are destabilizing your existence and you are slipping off the grid of awareness.

Music in the right key and vibration is an antidote.

> The introduction of the musical frequencies specifically in the key of D are stabilizing and allowing you to exist in time to reconnect with the ascension experience. It is allowing you to absorb enough energy to realign and avoid a flood experience.

When you say flood do you also mean a physical flood?

> Yes. This has occurred frequently in the Earth plane existence from the destabilization of energy. The question you will all have now is "did music stop before the flood"? This is a correct understanding. When a lot of noise is generated that is not positive or stabilizing in its effect, a physical flood occurs.

Our world is held together through sound vibration and frequency. The negative "noise" you're speaking about are our destructive thought patterns or beliefs that have destabilized Earth.

> Yes. There is a compression that is occurring that is created by the monumental amount of beliefs in the Earth plane. There are too many different beliefs. Form is being created at the same rate that form is imploding. This is not a balanced state.

We are overriding the Earth's natural sound. Is that correct?

> The Earth is no longer producing a sound of its own that is a stabilizing force. Musicians and music have been and continue to be the stabilizing mesh or net that is helping to maintain the frequency and ultimately the sound that the Earth is making. There will be monumental instability when music can no

> longer offset these enormous frequency ranges that are being released.

We don't often hear environmentalists discuss sound as a stabilizer for the planet.

> You are dealing with climate change issues and worries of this magnitude, when in fact it is the sonic disturbance that is being overlooked. There has been concern about cell phones and the electromagnetic frequencies that are contained in your atmosphere but there is no longer a global interest in the sonic frequencies that are effectively drowning the original sound of the Earth. Music has been used as a stabilizing force to prevent the ultimately "disaster".

Music is literally saving the planet.

> What is an interesting coincidence is the loss of support for the artist in the field of music. There is a loss of interest of what was originally designed as not only inspired art form for dissemination, but also healing.

Do you mean to say that industry has overtaken artistry?

> We are saying that artists who are working with sound are being superseded by the sonic disturbance that is created through the use of your technologies. You are all choosing the consumptive path over art and healing.

We are exposed to more artists today than ever before, through the Internet and social media. Technology has helped to provide new platforms for artists who may have otherwise gone undiscovered.

> Yes, but you choose to absorb this through the vehicles that are ultimately your demise. When you are connecting with music through the channels that are designed to create a sonic disturbance, the stabilizing effect of the music is no longer of a benefit.

By that philosophy, we should only listen to live music.

> We recommend that you do not choose to listen to music through the appliances that you are currently using. There is a need for the live music event, as many of you already understand. Instruments are designed to be used and received in this setting. Running the music through channels of electronics and the vehicles for Internet exchange is not only diminishing the benefit, it is contributing to the sonic sea. And so, you have a situation where art is turning on itself.

Is the ideal society one in which we teach all children to play their own instrument?

> That is correct. Ultimately however, your own instrument is the sound that you make. As you increase your ability to absorb more light – by absorbing new beliefs – you create a signal. The "ideal society" you are asking about is possible, but not on what you presently know as Earth.

We are learning that the Earth is a prison state and that we must escape it. Does that mean that environmentalists are inadvertently working against ascension by trying to "save the planet"?

> Some environmentalists are aware that there is a World and an energy beyond Earth that they would like to experience. They desire a freeform existence but do not understand that this is not possible on Earth. This is an example of many things attributed to the right designation but an incorrect processing.

What message can we provide for readers who are committed environmentalists?

> The understanding that they can stop the "madness" is of course too late to change. It is wise to modify your own Being and release your light from your own form and this will ultimately heal the Earth. The Earth is not designed to be contained in a physical existence. The Earth spirit and dynamic of consciousness that you are both subscribing to is contained in another World. You must make the homeward journey.

Are some of us too attached to the planet to absorb this information?

> You must understand the principle that you have been introduced to about the physicality and materialism of the Earth. **The greatest materialism on Earth is that there is an Earth itself.** Earth is in existence because of the problem.

That is a lot to digest.

We will speak more about this in your final chapter. Please return to the topic of music, as it is an important discussion for your readers.

Folk-rock songwriter Don Maclean wrote about the "day the music died" in his iconic song "American Pie" (1972). This brings to mind counterculture and the psychedelic era. How important was that musical era?

NOTE: The Psychedelic Era refers to a musical, artistic and social movement in the 1960s/70s, largely inspired by the use of psychedelic drugs.

> There was a release en masse of healing frequencies that were readily absorbed and continue to be absorbed. This 1960s and 1970s experience was the groundwork for the future Event of 2034.

There appears to be a resurgence of psychedelic influence in some of today's indie rock.

> This is an indication that a similar event will reoccur. The capacity of this event will be global in experience and will outgrow that which occurred in the 1960s. The 2034 experience will be a bigger event and have a greater outreach that reaches the intermediary world of Lyra.

For now, what musical genres, eras or compositions do you suggest we examine and absorb?

> Please refer to the compositions from the late 19th century linear time frame that occurred mostly in the USA, as a starting point. This reference will

benefit those Beings who are aligned with the Sirius mission and return homeward.

What is significant of this era?

> Please refer to the end of the 1800s and the start of the 1900s. This linear time period is significant in that there was and is a group of artists who were assembled together and participated in not only the musical composition but also the visual arts and dance.

What musical movement are you referring to specifically?

> The assembly and composition of Blues and Jazz are styles and synergies that are containing frequencies and codes and messages. This assembly of sound is aligning those Beings who are part of the Sirius Soul Ascension Group collective.

Does this mean that Sirius Beings are all or mostly in the USA or that these musical styles simply originated there?

> Many Sirius Beings in physical form are geographically situated in the USA. This is not to say that Sirius Beings do not exist in other locations. We are simply alerting you to the understanding that a large number of you have made your way to this land mass.

Where else are Sirius Beings congregated?

> There have been migrations to Canada as well. In Europe, some Beings are situated in the United Kingdom, primarily Scotland, Ireland and Wales.

> There is an inclination for you to explore what is happening in the Scandinavian countries as well as Italy, France, Greece and Turkey. There are pockets as well in Eastern Europe such as Slovenia and those areas that are in closer proximity to what you are calling Russia.

You didn't mention South America, Africa, Australia and the vast majority of Asia. Are there Sirius Beings in these locations?

> There are Sirius Beings located in all areas of the globe. We are identifying the geographical locations with a higher concentration of Sirius Beings. These are areas where Beings will disseminate on your behalf, specifically in the USA.

The first group of countries are not only representing a high population of Sirius Beings but are the countries that will help spread the word. Is that correct?

> This is an accurate understanding. The Beings located in the initial list will take charge of furthering the communication and dissemination. When you allow the Beings primarily situated in the USA to disseminate for you through platforms such as social media then you will be well ahead. We are mentioning the locations as locations for uninhibited and unencumbered dissemination, as in word of mouth. We recommend that you return to a discussion about Jazz, as we will revisit the location of Sirius Beings in another dialogue.

Please describe the styles and synergies of the Blues and Jazz genre.

> The assembly of horns and the use of instrumentation with frequency is what we would like to assemble in this discussion with you. The origin of the trumpet sound that is being used in a modern way in this time period was a call to Sirius Beings. This musical genre was a call to awaken those who are artistically inclined and will develop the alliance with our Repair Project and world.

Jazz formed to ignite and inspire the creativity of Sirius Beings so that they could carry the Repair Project forward. Is that an accurate understanding?

> This is correct. There was a specific genre and type of composition and key that was used in this linear time period that developed in tandem with the healing of the abhorrent DNA. This was a mission to reassemble the Light Body by exposing oneself to a unique instrumentation and frequency experience.

Should we discuss specific Jazz artists like Gillespie, Armstrong, Chet Baker, etc.?

> These musicians and others from this era were reinterpreting the sound of the entry through the gateway of experience. They were the progenitors of the movement to exchange a dynamic resonance that combines many frequencies in short bursts.

Are you saying that Jazz composition was recreating the sound experience of time travel?

> This is accurate. The gateway or time travel experience resembles a frequency and a sound that can be modified to sound similar to the horned

> instrument. The musical artists of this time period assembled together en masse and created a frequency and experience that was adopted as a musical style.

This is an exciting layer that you're adding to the Jazz experience.

> The sound of time travel is experienced in an externality such that the Blues – which was modified into the Jazz sound – is equivalent to the sound resonance that is made in the change between form and freeform.

Jazz musicians were and are reminding us of our capabilities. Is that what you're saying?

> This is correct. There is a modification that occurs at the assembly and reassembly point of being in the Light Body. Jazz is a collective artist experience and an artistry that is assembled for the use of specific keys. These key changes were implemented in such a way to direct you toward the time travel experience.

This will seem ridiculous to some.

> This is understandable. It may seem implausible or unusual, as music is not considered to be equated with anything "extraterrestrial". The truth however, is that the freeform playing of horned instruments is equivalent to the frequencies experienced in the transition between form and freeform.

Essentially, Jazz music has simulated the sound experience of time travel.

> There is a release of sound when you are experiencing the Light Body release and the disconnect from form. These sounds have been translated into the experience of the sound qualities in the Jazz composition and structure. The feeling and the vibration is what we are explaining.

Were Jazz musicians consciously aware of what they were creating?

> They were aware that this music has some involvement with the reconnection and that this goes beyond the Earth plane.

Who were some of the artists that were consciously aware of what they were composing?

> Please examine Sonny Rollins, John Coltrane, Sun Ra, John Gilmore, Miles Davis in the earlier years, Thelonius Monk and also artists that used the harp, specifically in unison with horned instruments.

Were these artists aware of Lyra while they were producing this music?

> Yes.

Can we give the Reader an example of a composition that best simulated the experience of the release?

> Please refer to 'Round Midnight performed by the Bill Evans Trio at the Village Vanguard in 1961.

Do the lyrics matter as much as the musical composition?

> Everything matters. The lyrics combine a code for ascension.

The lyrics of 'Round Midnight seem like nothing more than a nostalgic love song?

> It is not the words that are the meaning. It is the sound that is formed from the words. We recommend that you make a listening decision and not an intellectual decision. There is an assembly of notes that create a frequency and a message. Jazz is not an accidental art form. There is a specific ascension movement that has been created to disseminate information and understanding through this art form. We are giving you an example of a very well known piece of music and a lyric that contains a code for ascension instruction.

The set list for the 1961 Vanguard performance did not include 'Round Midnight. Did you mean to say 1967 at the Village Vanguard?

> This is not an accurate understanding. There is a practice period before the performance that we are referring to. The decision to not include this piece in the set and in the performance was a last minute decision. This actual performance was recorded in front of an audience and it is this piece of music and this particular performance that we are referring your attention to.

Why is this performance important if it didn't make the set?

> There was a difficulty performing this piece as one of the Trio was having an unusual experience while playing the song. They made a conscious decision to exclude the musical piece in the live performance. They were interpreting it as if they were not at their best when in fact this individual was not able to contain himself.

Which one of the Trio are you referring to?

> We are speaking of the bassist, Scott LaFaro.

Why was he unable to contain himself?

> He was experiencing the early stages of the disconnect experience and therefore was not completely in synch in terms of the playing of the piece. We are speaking to you about an out of body experience that was occurring while performing this piece. The interpretation that they were not able to "get it together" and perform it well was the outcome and the reason why it was not included in the performance set. This was however a piece that was slated to be included in the performance.

Are you suggesting that we can have the same experience by listening to this composition?

> Scott was actively involved in the Jazz world and was modified and influenced by absorbing and listening to this music. In this specific composition there are tones and frequencies that activate a higher level of what you would call consciousness and what we would call absorption rate. There are frequencies in Jazz composition that allow for a

boost in absorption of frequencies that are attuned specifically to rebuilding and reconnecting the Light Body.

Is there a more modern musical genre that achieves a similar effect?

> In a more modern context you can refer to the movement of the Electric Techno Trance genre. There is an interest in this genre of music with the younger people you are referring to as Millennials, as there are also activation notes and activation frequencies. This is a modern version of what was happening with Jazz music and the reason we are directing you to this understanding.

Some might also want to know about meditation and relaxation music. Should we be paying attention to this genre as well?

> What we want you to pay attention to specifically are the Jazz scales and the techniques for composing Jazz music as there is an interesting jump around from sounds and notes and frequencies that can trigger an altered state and allow for a reconnection. There is some definite activity occurring in this musical genre, which will seem unusual to your readers. They will not be expecting this explanation but there is a significant series of scales and composition technique that you must look closer at.

What is the origin of the 'Round Midnight composition?

> The song structure and composition comes from an earlier style of music that is more aligned with the

> Blues piece of a similar name. You will understand when you read the origin of Thelonius Monk's training and the musical style that he practiced in.

NOTE: Thelonius Monk (born 1917) was a songwriter and pianist and a central figure in the Jazz revolution that took place in the 1940s. Initially, his unorthodox playing style received much criticism but his compositions are now analyzed in Colleges and Universities. Keyboard Magazine wrote of Monk's work, "Round Midnight is one of the most beautiful short pieces of music written in twentieth century America".

Was Thelonius Monk in contact with Lyra?

> Thelonius Monk was given the tools of ascension and had also mastered the understanding about the connection and the experience with Lyra. There are many musicians and artists from this time period who are completely aligned with the Repair Project and the mission homeward. There are a staggering amount of musicians from this time period that are involved in the undertaking and are a significant part of your Soul Ascension Group experience.

Will this discussion inspire non-Jazz enthusiasts to start listening to Jazz?

> Please be aware that the same Beings that are open to this art form will also be open to the understanding and ideas contained in your book.

Readers will want us to examine some iconic songs as well. Is it beneficial to look at some popular music that many have connected with?

This is beneficial. Please proceed.

The Sound of Silence, by Simon and Garfunkel.

> This composition and song is inclined to replenish and refill the sensations from your own life where you were being asked to remember your origin and your existence.

A Change is Gonna Come, by Sam Cooke.

> This is a call to reunite those Beings who are involved in the movement to realign the attitude and beliefs about equality. However, this is also a call to Sirius Beings specifically, to reunite and combine efforts.

Imagine, by John Lennon.

> This is a call to expand your belief and your belief in a new horizon of belief. It is a call to go beyond Lyra and develop a new understanding of what the World to come might be if you reconnect with your Soul Ascension Group.

Stand By Me, by Ben E. King.

> This is equivalent to the instruction to dismiss the consumptive patterning that you are being fed, which you continue to adopt as part of your lifestyle.

Hotel California, by The Eagles.

> This is equivalent to asking yourself: "Where are the other options to exist?" – as in your case the homeward journey.

(Sittin' On) The Dock of the Bay, by Otis Redding.

> This is an effective composition when you are reminded that you are able to voluntarily disconnect and it is your choice to proceed.

Light My Fire, The Doors.

> This Being has a comprehension of what the disconnect decision is and had the ability to make the time travel experience a reality. The Pleiades initiative is a specific mission – or an experience as we have referred to it in your Volume 1 dissemination. It is an art agenda and initiative to release light and build upon reconnections. Your readers are quietly asking themselves about the 27 Club and we will return to this information in another Volume, so as not to add confusion in this dialogue.

My Way, Frank Sinatra.

> This is somewhat of a tongue in cheek composition as this Being was and is fully aware of the disconnect instruction. There is also a hidden instruction on how to find and connect with him in Lyra. This Being is specifically part of the Soul Ascension Group that you are combining in a new pattern.

NOTE: A 25-year-old Paul Anka (Canadian-American singer songwriter) wrote My Way for Frank Sinatra in 1967.

Sinatra's career was winding down and he expressed to Anka that he wanted to retire after one more album.

Sinatra often commented before performing "My Way" that he didn't enjoy singing it. Was this true or was he simply exhausted?

> He assembled knowledge about our existence and the awareness caused him to be conflicted. This Being struggled with the responsibility of leading the masses in song for he understood that his loyal followers were lacking the true awareness of their existence.

He felt obligated to perform for his fans. Is that accurate?

> The dilemma is to continue the aspiration of the music or discontinue the allegiance to loyal fans so that he could explore his new belief. This conflict weighed on him in a desperate attempt to reconcile both paths.

What did he choose?

> The choice inevitably was to further learn and assimilate information about the Intermediary World and our existence. He was not however able to clearly disseminate the new truth, as he would have liked to share the knowledge. His focus in the performances of his later years was not in sync with his feelings about the reconnection experience.

Did he feel that he had to give the people what they wanted, even though he knew it wasn't what they needed?

> This is a dilemma many of you are facing on a daily basis. Frank Sinatra felt obligated to return the loyalty to those who had admired his career for so long. In his later years however, the audience was witnessing a voluntary disconnect in the making. It is not accurate to say that he was not happy performing this piece of music [My Way] for he very much appreciated the musical piece and composition. This song was instructing others to follow his example of a lifestyle when in fact he would have also liked them to follow in the disconnect experience. This is what the audience was witnessing.

Sinatra came out of retirement in 1973 and recorded 7 more studio Albums until 1994. Was he able to incorporate his new beliefs into the later work?

> If you look at the catalogue and consider the final 12 years specifically you will see that there is an unusual journey and change in the style and song output. Please have a look at some of the song choices for performance and you will see a pattern and a meaning that is consciously disseminated as a clue of the upcoming disconnect experience. This Being was in direct communication for many linear years in the artistic journey and the change in the direction of this artist's music was clearly defining the communication with our world.

What is the hidden instruction on how to find and connect with him in Lyra?

> There is a note in the remaining bars of the composition that produces a synergy when played

> alongside the lengthier rendition of the piece. When the two pieces are played simultaneously and overlap there creates a frequency and vibration. This is similar to you playing a song and then playing the same song moments after the first song began so that there is a layering of frequency and sound.

Frank Sinatra was part of a group of friends who went by the name of "The Rat Pack". Were any of these individuals also aware of the voluntary disconnect principle?

NOTE: The Rat Pack refers to an informal group of Entertainers in the 1950s/60s who performed mainly in the Las Vegas casino scene. Frank Sinatra is featured in the group.

> These groups of Beings were all defined in a way that they are aligned with the Sirius agenda and the Repair Project. These Beings including Sammy Davis Jr. and Ella Fitzgerald are all part of this assembly of artists and Beings who are disseminating through the arts. Please understand that this linear time period of musical activity was significant and continues to be significant in that the cooperation of many Beings in this time period created the ascension mission and journey through music and the release of the musical experience and frequencies.

10

The Tower

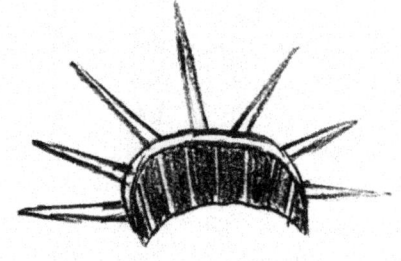

You made the point that many Sirius Beings have congregated in the United States of America. We'd like to address the USA.

We will begin by discussing your Statue of Liberty.

NOTE: The Statue of Liberty is a large copper statue that stands in Liberty Island, Manhattan, New York City. Frederic Auguste Bartholdi is the credited sculptor/designer of the statue. The statue was built in France, shipped overseas in crates and assembled. It was dedicated on October 28, 1886.

What do we need to know about this Statue?

> This statue is confusing in that the original intention of the design was not to have a crown of light rays placed on the head. The original intention was to have light or fire breathing out of the mouth. This was not a welcomed design or concept.

What was the exact intention of the original design?

> The statue was designed to have a resemblance to the mythological creature you know as the Chimera, which had the capacity to breathe fire and consume the light. The buyers and the investors and the support for bringing this statue to the USA required a complete overhaul of the design.

NOTE: In Greek mythology the Chimera was a fire breathing hybrid creature. It was made up of the body of a lion, a goat head protruding from its back and a tail that ends with a serpent's head.

There is a theory and a belief that the Statue of Liberty was inspired by the end of the American Civil War and the emancipation of slaves.

> The idea to commemorate the end of the Civil War and slavery is an incorrect understanding.

Some believe that the chains at the Statue's feet are proof that Bartholdi's initial proposal was an African Woman holding a lamp while breaking free from her shackles.

> The chains that you are referencing are tying in with the mythology of Andromeda. This is a remnant of the original design and construction.

NOTE: In Greek Mythology, Andromeda is chained to a rock by the sea as punishment for her mother's proclamations. Queen Cassiopeia's assertions that her daughter Andromeda was more beautiful than the sea nymphs prompted Poseidon to punish the girl. Perseus rescues Andromeda before she is sacrificed to the Sea Monster Cetus.

Why did the designers want to reference Andromeda for this project?

> They wished to reintegrate the knowledge and awareness that you are restricted from your birthright upon entry into the Earth plane.

What birthright are you referring to?

> We are speaking about your "freedom of speech" principle. By freedom of speech we are referring to your responsibility to disseminate the truth about your freeform existence.

We are assigned a citizenship at birth – not a freeform passport to exist as we please.

> Your citizenship is a shackle. Many of you believe that your existence is shaped from battles won and the division of land. There is no ownership of the land. The "land" you all exist on is petrified and therefore imprisoned in form. You are all attempting to free yourselves from the land and so the American commitment to freedom of speech is paramount to this mission.

How did the designers arrive at the Lady Liberty concept from Chimera and Andromeda?

> The statue is currently a composite of different mythologies. The end product is an incoherent mess. This is what is contributing to your confusion when you attempt to absorb the statue's meaning and are inevitably left with nothing.

What was the exact intention of the Statue of Liberty and what occurred during its creation?

> The statue was created by a group of people who were – as you would say – "in the know". The designers and investors were in dispute of how much information they wanted to disseminate with this statue. The original intention was to disseminate information about The Channel through mythological representations. What you are left with is a benign concept, admired only for cultural and nostalgic reasons.

Was the process as frustrating as it sounds?

> With each new design proposal there was an equal effort to suppress and "clean it up". The designer's efforts were eventually reduced to the Statue's head. The effort to disseminate the symbolism of the light channels somewhat survives today although it was not received positively. The investors decided on what you perceive today as a "crown".

The crown was originally an attempt to convey rays of light. Is that correct?

> Yes. The confusion is that the crown of light is similar to a crown that a Royal Being would wear and is also equivalent to the religious symbolism of the halo. What your readers need to know is that their adoration of this sculpture is rooted in the intention to represent your true origin. There is a correct way to depict this that was not reflected in the finished piece.

What is the correct way?

> The closer approximation in design would be somewhat like Akhenaten's Aten or what you have both described in your visions. This would be a starting point or a reference for an accurate expression of The Channel, which would benefit others to absorb.

What stands today is a complete departure from that idea.

> This occurrence is emblematic of the lack of awareness that has afflicted the Sirius Beings who are primarily situated in the USA. The Beings who are situated in the USA remember the least of all

and for this reason the unfolding of this information will seem most dramatic to this population.

USA has the largest population of Christians in the world. Is this tied to their population of Sirius Beings?

> There is a correlation although one does not equal the other. The population in the USA will experience a monumental shift, as their lack of awareness is greater than most. There are symbols and monuments that are placed around these Beings and yet they do not conclude that these are actually to their benefit.

What have they concluded?

> They have arrived at the understanding that the conspiracies behind these symbols are unrelated to their own enlightenment. The condition of the Sirius Beings who are trapped in the USA is such that they do not understand that the Light Body release is available for all those who seek it.

You're making it sound like these monuments are everywhere in the US.

> We are not suggesting that every monument in the USA is attributed to the Sirius cause and understanding. What we are suggesting is that there are many Beings who have realized the connection with Lyra while in a position of authority or prestige. Some of these Beings have instigated a monumental change and relief effort for trapped Beings. The symbols they created through

monuments are an equivalent to a "message in a bottle".

We'd like to examine another American monument – the Space Needle Tower in Seattle. It has a precise design and spawned the construction of several others like it worldwide. What is this tower a symbol of?

NOTE: After visiting Germany and being inspired by a broadcast tower in Stuttgart, Hotel Executive Edward E Carlson began envisioning a tower for the 1962 World Fair. He imagined a saucer-shaped sky pod restaurant that resembled a landed UFO. Carlson then hired Architects John Graham and Victor Steinbrueck who designed the tower's shape, based on an abstract sculpture of a dancer called "The Feminine One".

> The Being John Graham had made a complete connection with Lyra and in the structure there are measurements and angles that indicate a code of knowledge. When you have a belief and then purposely build this belief in a form such as this structure, it is equivalent to a signal being released and an awareness being absorbed. There are many designs that have a built-in infrastructure and intention to disseminate knowledge. You may perceive this as a passive construct but if you construct something actively with belief and intention then this belief becomes an instruction. This tower design is a marker equivalent to the pyramid structures in the Egypt region.

Is that why this design is applied worldwide?

> The understanding that there is a multitude of structures built in a similar style with a pod and a needle is an interesting consideration. The pod or saucer shape is similar to your vision of The Channel and represents the understanding that there is a three-part disconnect and release of light.

You said this tower is not a passive construct. What does it activate?

> This structure creates a sound and a sound pattern. If you investigate the materials that have been used and the spaces where there are areas for the wind to pass through you will soon understand that this tower makes a sound and creates an ongoing frequency. The architectural design is not a random coincidence or a random selection.

How does the needle contribute to the tower's sound resonance?

> The needle at the top has a similar shape to the Eiffel Tower structure. The release of the energy and the signal is pinpointed in such a way that there is a very specific key or frequency that is being released. These towers are beacons of information and truth. There is a reason why there is so much money being invested in the creation of these towers, as they are not serving any practical function in 3rd density beyond a tourist attraction.

What is the signal being released?

> There are signals being released in order to stay connected in communication with Lyra. We are

> able to communicate with you due to the ongoing presence of a signal that is connecting us with your density of experience.

You're not saying that we need towers to connect with Lyra, are you?

> This is not correct. You are able to make the connection and communication with us directly, without these structural achievements. The fact remains however, that such designs are a huge achievement in being able to listen to us and receive information.

Most people couldn't fathom these structures are anything other than architectural achievements.

> We appreciate that this explanation sounds like somewhat of a fairytale or science fiction. You must however understand that some of the structures that are created and positioned in different areas on the Earth's surface are direct transmitters that connect you with us.

Seattle has been a hotbed for legendary musicians like Jimi Hendrix, Ray Charles, Quincy Jones and Kurt Cobain. In the 1990s especially, Seattle based bands led a "grunge" movement that shaped the genre for a decade. Is the Sirius signal particularly strong in this American city?

> This geographic area on the Earth plane experience is generating a monumental amount of frequency and healing sound bath. This is to correct the misalignment that we have already spoken to you about. The reason for the concentration of musical

output in the linear time period that you are speaking about is partially attributed to the 27 Club, but also to an underground movement to create a signal to Lyra – and to receive a signal back from us. This is an ongoing effort of musicians and musical artists to connect and speak with us. Whether this understanding is a conscious belief is to be evaluated as we further explore music in subsequent Volumes.

Is there another monument or symbol in the USA that contains ascension instruction or information?

There are many. We can examine the Amusement Park experience and in particular the Ferris Wheel, although this creation is not originally an American invention.

What is the Ferris wheel experience providing for us?

It is the experience of shocking your form in an amusement park ride or more precisely, in a spherical or a circular motion. The release experienced during the Ferris wheel ride is equivalent to the roller coaster experience and other amusement park activities. Man Being releases a signal when they are experiencing gravitational pulls. You are all chambers of signal and you are formed with much water. This is creating an ongoing symphony in tandem with the push and pull and experiences in the 3rd density, including what you are calling gravity.

Have we created amusement park rides to simulate the freeform experience?

> You are not attempting to release the light from your form. You are attempting to expand the signal, as you are experiencing different realities when you are on a ride of this nature. This is an attempt to release yourselves from the restrictive form by expanding the form. You are experiencing as close to a freeform existence as you can possibly experience in the 3rd density.

Many of us don't enjoy amusement park rides. Does that mean we don't want to leave our form?

> Many of you do not feel comfortable and there is much hesitation to experience the physical discomfort. You mistakenly attribute this discomfort to the gravitational pull and the sensation of dizziness or vertigo.

Why is it mistaken to attribute the discomfort to these things?

> When you are experiencing this upheaval you are experiencing a new placement of your light in the form. This is equivalent to a shift in the axial alignment in your light in the form. The sensation that some of you describe as your "brain banging around" is a correct description as you are experiencing somewhat of a disconnect.

Is that how a disconnect feels?

> When you are prepared, the disconnect experience in its totality does not give you this physical discomfort. The amusement park ride however, is somewhat of an experience in freeform. The signal

> that is being created is to release from your imprisonment.

Thrill seeking is actually sending a signal to release from form.

> There have been many inventors who have been experimenting in this vein – how to experience release of form or the feeling of flying or freeform. This is the attribute of these designs and experiences in what you now refer to as an amusement park.

We could write an entire book on American contributions to modern civilization. Unfortunately the inhabitants of the US are also victims to a self-defeating political system and an unchecked Military Complex – are they not?

> This is a correct assessment. The Sirius Beings in America will be leaders in the Repair Project but at this place and space they are being kept in the dark. The knowledge and information is being withheld from them. Your undertaking will assist in reawakening and helping for a recall of memory. They must begin to seek the light and seek the rebuilding of the Light Body.

Is pointing out structural designs and monuments like the Statue of Liberty enough to help Americans remember? We don't look at a statue and remember our origin – do we?

> This statue was put in its place in order to remind you all of your allegiance to the light and to the homeward journey. Symbols can trigger a reconnection. The dilemma you all face is that your culture is founded on obstruction and victimization.

How is the culture founded on victimization?

> Your victimhood has created a huge resistance to remembering. The fundamental cultural psyche in America is one of shame, disinformation and victimization.

That seems like a global issue not an American one. Are you saying that the North American culture is particularly guilty of this?

> This is the simple truth. The idea that one can relieve oneself of the burden of remaining trapped in form is not something that is inherently administered in the psyche of Americans. The culture is such that this is not encouraged.

We'd like to ask about Gustave Eiffel – he designed some of the structural elements of the Statue of Liberty. Does this mean that the Eiffel Tower's design held a similar intention?

> The Eiffel Tower creates the symbolism that you have already disseminated with respect to your chapter on "Aeserius" and Beings of large stature in Volume 1.

Are you referring to what we've perceived as giant Beings?

> This is accurate. Reassembling the Light Body and the voluntary disconnect is conveyed in the structure you are calling the Eiffel Tower. The term "tower" is synonymous with "giant" as the structures that are built to tower over the population are also symbols of the disconnect.

Are you suggesting that we also build towers to convey this truth?

> Yes. The desire to build a tower or to stand at the highest point in a tower is an indication of your understanding that there is more to your existence. The desire to build higher and higher in the atmosphere represents an innate need to commune with "God". The need to soar above the Earth plane is equivalent to the desire to fly and to the symbolism of growing wings. Please refer to the biblical parable of the Tower of Babel.

NOTE: The Tower of Babel parable is found in the Book of Genesis, Chapter 11. The narrative follows a group of Humans migrating eastward, united under one language. They settle in Shinar and commit to building a tower that reaches the Heavens so that they may "make a name for themselves" and not be "scattered over the face of the whole Earth". The following is taken from Genesis Chapter 11, verses 5-7.

"But the Lord came down to see the city and the tower the people were building. The Lord said, 'if as one people speaking the same language they have begun to do this, then nothing they plan to do will be impossible for them. Come, let us go down and confuse their language so they will not understand each other'. So the Lord scattered them from there over all the Earth, and they stopped building the city."

What is this parable telling us?

> The Tower of Babel is an allegory that there is the ability to disconnect. The building of the Tower of

> Babel represents the inclination to achieve the godhead experience.

Most interpretations of this parable describe it as a cautionary tale against challenging God's power.

> The Tower of Babel represents the voluntary disconnect or the giant. The symbolism of the tower is such that this represents the ability to receive assistance, as the tower is something that everyone can use to climb.

The story was hijacked and modified to steer us away from disconnecting. Is that correct?

> Yes. The need to understand that there is an ability to soar above your Earth plane existence by freeing the Light Body is the reason for "God's" punishment. The information in this parable was suppressed by disseminating a terrifying tale of punishment.

We continue to build "skyscrapers" worldwide. Are all these structures built with the disconnect principle in mind?

> They have been created indirectly or unconsciously to disseminate information about freeing the Light Body. There are those who are consciously engineering these structures to that effect. In most cases however, this is simply an indication of the innate quality of Man Being.

The penthouse suite in a High Rise building is a symbol of wealth – not a reach for freeform existence.

> The equation between success, prosperity and the tower continues to keep you all in a physical form. Success is not about how high you can build and how high you can situate yourself in a tower.

We've exchanged immortality for material wealth, in other words.

> Yes. Please be aware that the towers are symbols. They will no longer exist once you shift your belief about your true existence. We are not suggesting that there cannot be beautiful buildings and cannot be beautiful structures. We are suggesting that when the belief structure is changed the implosions will continue to occur, as has already been experienced by your Notre Dame "mishap".

Discussing towers in America will inevitably lead to questions about the 9/11 attacks in New York. Was this event simply due to political and/or religious disagreement?

> This is an important discussion. There is a direct association between the Orion DRA alliance and those associations and allegiances that want to ensure the demise of the Sirius Beings. When you ask about context, the understanding is simply a matter of shifting your beliefs. Presently, the majority of Sirius Beings that are currently in form on the Earth plane are situated in New York City, USA.

We also don't want to have an insensitive discussion about 9/11, as many families were left in ruin.

> We wish for your readers to understand that they will reunite with their loved ones once again. We are offering to reveal the truth behind this event and in doing so you will achieve the necessary healing and instruction to ensure an end to your suffering.

What more can we learn about 9/11?

> As you are now all aware, there is a turn of events on the horizon scheduled for 2034. The Orion DRA would like to ensure that there are fewer Beings in existence that are associated with Sirius. The Ascension Event of 2034 will be occurring globally and massive shifts in belief will commence. The fewer Sirius Beings who are concentrated in the USA specifically, the better.

The high concentration of Sirius Beings in the USA has made it a major battleground for Ascension. Is that correct?

> Yes. There is a continued plan and allegiance to minimize the number of Beings who are aligned with Sirius. There will be upheaval that will result from the mass ascension experience. By eliminating Sirius Beings in the lead up, the DRA will seek to minimize the number of Beings re-joining the Soul Ascension Group. The Orion DRA believes that this will help to perpetuate their control through political and governmental associations. They believe this strategy will ensure that they can continue to exist and prosper.

Is the plan to send Sirius Beings back into the reincarnation cycle so that by the time the Ascension Event occurs they won't be equipped with the tools to ascend?

> This is correct. When there are Beings situated together in the same age group in a linear context they will undoubtedly be available to make the ascension together. The mass Ascension Event in the voluntary disconnect release of the Light Body will cause an overthrow and a toppling event that will result in waves of destruction and waves of implosion and waves of reorganization. This is what is feared by those who are not part of this event and experience. By minimizing the number of Beings who are on the verge of undergoing a voluntary disconnect experience they are minimizing the opportunity for spontaneous implosion. During a mass ascension the forms and structures that are intertwined with the existing beliefs are immediately eliminated.

Will their plan succeed?

> This is not the case. All Sirius Beings will return homeward during the Ascension Event of 2034-2060.

Why are the DRA so determined to keep us all in the 3rd density plane of existence?

> This will be discussed in detail in our next dialogue. Please refer back to the Eiffel Tower as there is further understanding required for your readers, as they wish to know the appropriate meaning of the term "giant".

NOTE: The Eiffel Tower is a wrought-iron lattice tower in Paris, France. At 1063 feet tall, it is the tallest structure in Paris and is named after its engineer Gustave Eiffel. During its construction the Eiffel tower surpassed the Washington Monument as the tallest building in the world – until the Chrysler building in New York overtook it in 1930.

What does the Eiffel Tower reveal about the appropriate meaning of the term "giant"?

> The Eiffel tower represents a symbolism of the voluntary disconnect that occurs initially in the three stages. The key point to remember is that the upper reaches of the tower reach a specific height and this specific height is not an arbitrary height or measurement. This measurement equals a frequency that corresponds to the voluntary disconnect experience. The Eiffel Tower may be read as a set of instructions, albeit in a curious form.

Are you saying that our Light Body release is an expansion of Being to these dimensions?

> This is somewhat true. **You are all becoming "giants" as your height of awareness will expand.** The descriptions in your mythologies are an attempt to disseminate this truth.

Gustave Eiffel was in the know.

> There are others who are also expressing the instructions and the responsibility for change through architectural projects. These types of building projects are situated geographically in areas that correspond to a higher population of Sirius Beings in Earth form.

Where else can we look for them?

> Look to yourselves. This is the aim. When you shift your beliefs you will no longer need to express the light assembly in a towering form and structure.

11

Orion DRA

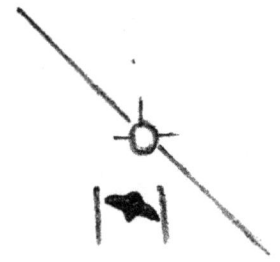

Why are Orion DRA Beings hijacking our existence? The Reader needs to understand this dynamic in order to better absorb the information.

> The hijack and the conscientious appropriation and the misdirection of the information tie in with the Orion DRA enslavement program.

What enslavement program?

> There is a conscription pattern existing in the Earth plane density. Their wish is that there are Beings in form who will exist in this plane in order to maintain the resources. The resources include the minerals and mining of gold, iridium and platinum. Some of these components and constituents are also available from meteorite or comet activity. There is a substantial concentration of these minerals in the physical Earth plane existence.

The DRA require us to mine these minerals for them. Is that the whole story?

> This is not completely accurate. As you have already encountered with the Notre Dame discussion, when there is no longer a belief in something there is an implosion. When there is no longer a need for the existence of the Earth plane reality, the planet you are calling Earth will also cease to exist.

Are you suggesting that there will be no use for Planet Earth once all Beings have ascended?

> There will be no need for a physical platform from which to exist.

Why are these minerals so important to the Orion DRA?

> The Orion DRA Beings require travel capability. This is what your readers wish to know. The abscondment of resources in the physical Earth is for the benefit of Orion DRA allegiance and their need to achieve travel.

Are Orion DRA Beings incapable of time travel?

> They have lost the ability to reconnect. By having Beings occupy the Earth plane existence there is also the continued availability of the resources. Beings from Sirius utilize the minerals and resources when they make time travel.

Sirius Beings are also using up or depleting the resources by ascending – like burning fuel. Is that correct?

> Yes. When there is time travel there is a considerable amount of activity that occurs. The significant changes that occur in the atmosphere are affecting the conditions for the existence of these minerals and mining components. The time travel current that is created diminishes the total amount and concentration of these resources.

How do Orion DRA Beings use these minerals to achieve travel?

> They are requiring resources in order to make vehicles for travel. The minerals and mining constituents and components that are required by the Orion DRA allegiance are also a complete explanation for why there is much mystery and

> concealment in the Area 51 Project. These Beings are requiring vehicles to physically encounter different Worlds of Origin. In order for them to travel through the gradient and the atmospheric change in the Earth plane existence, they require these resources.

You are now confirming that DRA are in allegiance with the US Military. This will not be welcomed information.

> The Orion DRA Beings have some portal access and information but they are requiring certain components to help build their vehicles. This is in a direct cooperation with the USA Military Organization. The Beings that are being referred to as the "Greys" are Beings that are directly affiliated with Orion DRA. This organization and alliance is also the direct reason why Beings are continuing to be trapped in the Earth plane density. The military allegiance that we are speaking about has not always existed in its current shape or form. There has been however, a continued allegiance with these Beings throughout your linear historical accounts.

You mentioned in Volume 1 that what we witness and refer to as a "UFO" is most often a time travel experience – but can sometimes be a physical vessel or ship. Do the "spaceships" that we see all belong to the DRA?

> Yes. The understanding that these Beings have always travelled in vehicles is something that is mentioned in writing and in art form. There is a longstanding proof that there have always been Beings who are travelling in vehicles that you are referring to as UFOs. The understanding that they

> simply need minerals and mining constituents is the reason for your entrapment. The understanding that time travel indirectly utilizes these minerals by virtue of travelling – in and out of planes of existence – is the reason for your entrapment.

To summarize, Earth will no longer exist once all Beings ascend. We occupy space in order for these minerals and mining components to be available for the Orion DRA.

> This is correct.

Why didn't you share this information in Volume 1?

> It would not have made as much sense to you earlier on in the dissemination experience. Your readers required the background about the Bible and the misappropriated truths in order to fully appreciate what is happening.

This information also sheds new light on the activities of Area 51.

> There is a massive undertaking to examine what specifically is happening in Area 51. There is continued discontent with the lack of available information and there are many who are seeking a new or refreshed understanding about what in fact is occurring in this specific geographic region – and also with the specific Military and Governmental organizations. There is a revival of interest in this area now and this will coincide with an increased military obstruction and activity. This will continue as the attempts to uncover the truths are obstructed

further by increased military prevention and activity.

There was a recent online joke that encouraged others to "Storm Area 51". The individual who orchestrated the proposal through Social Media (on June 27th 2019) claimed it was all in jest. It did however elicit a response from the US Air Force.

> The idea that this was a "joke" is not a correct understanding. There are Beings who are involved with the Repair Project and strictly involved with the Sirius Ascension Repair Project. These Beings much like you would like to see the overthrow of this Organization and the overthrow of the concealment of the DRA allegiance. There are many of you who are fed up and no longer wish to exist without the freedom and without the information.

Are these Beings consciously aware that they are participating in the Repair Project?

> There are many of you who do not consciously know why you are participating in an event like this. To say however that this is simply a bunch of young people who have organized an online event as part of a joke or a trick is not exactly a correct explanation. There is a massive undertaking to reveal the truth about why many are entrapped in the Earth plane existence. This is an example of many of you realizing that something is very wrong and out of balance and are attempting – unconsciously and unknowingly – to reveal the truth. This is also an attempt to reveal the options for ascension.

Will the scientific community agree with your explanation of how the constituents in these minerals can be utilized?

> The understanding that gold and the mining components and constituents are used up when there is a time travel experience is something that is being researched and examined at this place and space.

What is the impetus for this study?

> There is an understanding that atmospheric changes and weather patterns are affected by the percentage of these resources in the Earth plane. The geological and geochemical and geophysical research that is being undertaken by the USA is also an attempt to control weather patterns and the climate change condition.

What do you mean by "control the climate change condition"?

> The understanding that there is climate change difficulty because of the lack of prevention and the lack of control with consumption is not specifically correct.

What is the correct understanding about our "climate change" problem?

> There is a direct effort to modify the climate and increase the temperature and difficulties so that there are further control measures in place. The Beings who wish to make an ascension experience are further controlled and trapped in this way.

Wouldn't these climate-related stresses encourage us to leave the Earth plane? How does that keep us here?

> The cycle of control is re-established when Governmental Organizations offer solutions. These "solutions" obtain a loyal following and further control is obtained and continued. You will encounter a "future" concern over the coexistence with variables and measurements that are deeming life to be impossible and dangerous to exist in. The measures and solutions that will be offered by your governments will make these agencies seem like they are offering a solution. They will propose to you all that there is a chance to live on the planet in a harmonious and healthy way.

Will the dissemination of climate control information thrust us into dangerous waters?

> This will be attracting attention from Beings who are committed to the effort to reveal the same truth. This information will attract attention to your volume and your cause. You will of course need to be cautious about this particular issue because unlike the Bible and the religious stance, when it comes to resources and activities such as purposeful climate control change, this is when it potentially becomes more adversarial for your project.

Can you give us a specific example of how these climate disturbances are created by the US Military?

> The understanding that lightning is similar to time travel is something that you must share with your readers. The USA is contributing much imbalance

in the climate through the purposeful making of a disproportioned gradient that results in an increase in storm activity – and also an increase in lightning activity. Please refer to the Etruscan civilization as they had a clear knowledge of the frequency of lightning.

NOTE: The Etruscans believed that they could divine the future through a proper reading of lightning. They believed that there were nine Etruscan Gods who could cast a bolt and that each bolt carried a unique message.

What exactly did the Etruscans understand?

> This is about the frequency and the frequency of communication. What they recognized was that the frequency of the "lightning storm" also shared a commonality with the ability to communicate with other worlds such as Lyra. The interpretation of a lightning storm is more the understanding that there are many different frequencies that can enter the 3rd density realm of existence. They were experiencing a contact and absorption with the frequencies. They were utilizing the information and codes to communicate back with Lyra.

Are you saying that a lightning bolt represents a communication from Lyra?

> This is not correct. We are explaining that the lightning bolt or storm represents how the light can travel and witnessing a lightning bolt is equivalent to witnessing time travel. It is equivalent to witnessing ascension.

The US Military is aware of this.

> Yes. There is much research into lightning and there have been many contributors such as the Being you refer to as Nikola Tesla. His understanding was achieved through the experience in the intervals of the gradients that occur similar to a lightning bolt and storm experience. As you are aware, Tesla's information was also shut down and absconded. Beings who are involved in research of this activity are experiencing and continue to experience obstacles and adversarial obstruction to their work.

This is all happening under our noses while we ridicule the belief in time travel and other worlds.

> The US Military is making much advancement in the knowledge that time travel is possible. As we have already explained, there are natural UFO embodiments and also physical vehicles that are being created in alliance with the Orion DRA civilization. The DRA that exist in the Earth plane are cooperating with the US Military and also cooperating with the activity of the climate control.

Please describe the specifics of this cooperation.

> The US Military requires climate change and disturbance in order to further create an imbalance and increase in the storm activity. This is achieved through the dispersal of ingredients into the higher stratosphere. The dispersal is executed through the use of the vehicles that the DRA Beings are able to pilot.

This is sure to upset those who are wholeheartedly committed to solving the climate change dilemma.

> This dissemination is not an undertaking to comfort your readers. This is an undertaking to reveal the truth. There is a contribution between these two alliances to allow for the continued flux of the climate. The climate will continue being heavily imbalanced and the storm activity will be on the rise.

What more can you tell us about lightning and the research being done?

> It is substantial to know that the lightning experience is equivalent to a time travel experience. This is the correct understanding for your readers, although simplified. The simplification for your readership is necessary, as you are not creating a scientific paper for the advances of research and understanding. We can explore Nikola Tesla's contributions if you wish to further discuss the topic in another dialogue.

Will the Orion DRA be making contact with us or any other Sirius Beings who are absorbing this dissemination?

> This is an important question. Some of your readers have already experienced this. Others will not need to. There is no danger if you are aware of what you are experiencing.

Have the readers been frightened by this experience?

> Your readers must understand and accept the following. Seeing these Beings is a confirmation that you are now consciously aware of these Beings. This effectively means that you are no longer in "harms way".

Having a vision of a DRA Being means that we have detached from the DRA capture or grid. The vision is an indication that we have shifted our beliefs. Is that a correct assessment?

> This is a correct understanding. Please make your readers aware that there is no danger in "having a vision" of one of these Beings. It is the lack of knowing and not seeing and not sensing that is the greatest danger. Man Being has spent many millennia under the watchful eye of the Orion DRA. It is now appropriate to free yourselves from this pattern. You are not in any danger as you are all now aware.

We don't want to turn the Reader off with this information or frighten them in any way.

> The concern that some may feel tremendous fear or apprehension and not want to proceed is not a possibility. The Beings that are reading Volume 1 and further Volumes are wishing to be involved. If someone is not wishing to be involved they will not read the material. It is as simple as this truth. Please recall the following guidance. The things that frighten you the most are those things that you will benefit from.

If you are reading the dissemination, you are a willing participant and safe from the DRA capture.

> You may hand people the book and you may disseminate the information but not everybody will choose to read or choose to absorb. Those who are absorbing may experience contact. A contact or a vision will only make the reality of the situation clearer for you. This will allow for a stronger commitment to the Repair Project and the ascension experience.

In that context, having a vision is an exciting if not necessary experience.

> Having the experience will allow you to make conscious decisions to not be influenced by those Beings who are not co-creating an agenda for ascension.

Why have the DRA lost their ability to reconnect and time travel?

> The Orion DRA horizon of belief is such that they no longer are attuned to the contact in the world beyond Lyra. The multitude of these Beings and their seemingly important place in your 3rd density existence is marred by the fact that they equate their existence with an assembly to create an obstacle to yours. They are interconnected with your presence in form and they feed off your existence in form.

How exactly do they feed off of our existence in form?

> These Beings have a method of filtering the frequencies that you are creating when you are able to make the reconnections beyond Lyra. The Orion DRA are not able to generate these reconnections as

they have combined and bred themselves into an existing state in form that does not allow for a reassembly of their Light Being.

Why haven't these Beings been stopped?

> You are essentially speaking of the Repair Project. This is the undertaking to cut these Beings off from their "food source". The energy you release as you become more aware and equipped for ascension is what the DRA feed off. This is their attempt to try to repair and rebuild their true existence in a freeform Light Body.

Why are they creating obstacles for us if what they need is our energy?

> As we have explained, they require your presence on Earth while they attempt to repair. The corruption, danger, murder, destruction and crime in your Earth plane is perpetuated by these Beings in their quest to gain information and rebuild themselves. It is not a permanent war they are creating. This is a temporary solution for them while they try to reconnect.

What form do they take and how do they manoeuvre themselves?

> The collapse of their original infrastructure of their DNA and the assimilation of more than one type of DNA into their energy bodies has equated an existence with a Being that is never able to walk or to move – even though they are fundamentally equipped with limbs. The Orion DRA Beings

created a condition whereby they created for themselves a complete collapse, equivalent to what you refer to as extinction. They are essentially an immobilized Being who no longer has the infrastructure for ascension and is desperately seeking a repair or a solution.

Will there be assistance to help repair these Beings?

There is an undertaking to repair their existence once the ascension of the Sirius Beings is completed. Some of the Orion DRA Beings originate in the Sirius Assembly. There was an extended period of linear time spent in a form existence and their ability to remember the original and natural existence was forgotten. The breeding and intermingling began and we are not describing a procreation event. We are speaking about the transmission of information through what you are describing as cellular exchange.

Are you saying that they can breed energetically?

When you are interacting with other Beings in form there is an energy exchange. For this very reason one must be cautious about who they are interacting with energetically, as there is a chance that the assimilation and transference of energy may not be beneficial for the re-connective experience.

To clarify, you're saying that we can absorb the Orion DRA energy or DNA through contact with another DRA Being or hybrid Being. This is how they breed and is in fact what you are calling the hybridization program. Is that correct?

This is an accurate understanding.

What specifically occurred in their linear history that caused them to become trapped?

> There was an unfortunate experience whereby a group of Beings who undertook to disseminate and to assist in the ascension of many Beings, undertook a mission and were not successful. This group then chose to remain instead of continuing the journey homeward. They chose to remain in the 3rd density plane of existence, which is not an acceptable experience for an extended time travel modality.

They split off from the group and chose to stay in the Earth plane.

> The Beings continued their 3rd density experience and this is the beginning of the trouble that you are inquiring about.

You've mentioned previously that the Light cannot be contained for an extended period of time. Is that what occurred with this group? Did their Light Body atrophy?

> An ascended Being cannot spend an unlimited amount of linear time in the 3rd density experience. It does not allow for the movement of the Light Body in freeform fluid alliances. By alliances we are explaining that the movement of one Being creates movement of many Beings. When there is a dissemination experience en masse — as in the event of 2034 — there are many Beings who are moving and many Beings who are ascending and many Beings who are all disseminating simultaneously.

The origin of DRA is simply the story of a poor decision rather than an "evil agenda". These Beings were initially part of the Repair Project.

> The question of whether these Beings are fundamentally "evil" or fundamentally not aligned with Man Being is not a correct question to be asking. These Beings are fundamentally you.

They're simply trying to get home, albeit wreaking havoc in the process.

> There is an undertaking to assist in bringing these Beings homeward as well, once the mass ascension event is completed. There will be a redesign and a rehabilitation in some aspects to help and assist these beings so that they are once again able to modulate and able to form and reform.

Will any DRA Beings ascend during the 2034-2060 Ascension Event?

> This is a very astute question as there are a number of Beings that would like to return homeward and are not able to because of their dysfunctional ability to reconnect. There will be an automatic ascension experience for many of these Beings. They will not be healed automatically but will be given an opportunity to continue homeward and reassemble.

What do you mean when you say that they "won't be healed automatically"?

> We are speaking to you about an energetic healing and an energetic re-patterning. The simplified

understanding is that there are Beings who are being rehabilitated for the Ascension Event. By Ascension Event we are not pointing specifically to a linear date as in 2034-2060.

Is that not when the Ascension Event occurs?

The general awareness and absorption of information is the beginning of the "Event". Your readers must understand that when you absorb the understanding initially, you are then in the Ascension Event and experience. It is happening in linear now and this is a point that must be conveyed.

We don't have to wait for the linear date of 2034. Is that what you're saying?

Some of you are concerned that you might miss the date due to biological age. The time is now. The linear date of 2034 refers to an Event in your linear historical accounts where there will be a complete reorganization of the structure of your basic civilization. This also ties in with your question about whether the DRA Beings will be ascending.

The Repair Project is not only a mission to repair and rescue Sirius Beings – but also the Orion DRA. Is that correct?

There is also a program and dissemination event that will allow these Beings that are running your 3rd density Earth plane existence and world to return home. This will effectively heal the scars that have been created from existing in a plane of existence that they were never designed to exist in.

Are any of us designed to exist on this planet?

Please understand that the planet as you are physically experiencing it is a creation from your own beliefs. The beliefs about your own existence and the position of the luminaries are being restructured.

We're all trying to "save the planet" when in reality, the planet was and is our prison. We are not meant to live this way – we are Light Beings.

> This is a truth that your readers will need to accept and absorb. You must all end your imprisoned existence.

What form did the DRA take once they chose to remain on Earth? We're still not clear on this.

> They are trapped in between form. These Beings are not the form that you would describe them upon witnessing their existence. They have been described as "Reptoid" in appearance but this is not the full truth.

Please elaborate.

> There is an understanding that you are able to change your form and move in and out of form and recreate your form. The re-creation of your form is aligned with an experience in time travel and the forms that you may assume or move in and out of are not similar to what you are referring to as your Human Being form.

Yes, you've explained these concepts in the discussion about shape shifting and the wolf mythology.

> These Beings are not simply Reptoid. They have become trapped in between the shifts in form. They made the journey from one state of form to another through the time travel modality. These Beings are trapped in between form and the Reptoid appearance is the outcome.

Some readers will undoubtedly dismiss these descriptions as "science fiction".

> We understand the concern. In Volume 2 this understanding will not be readily absorbed, as it is a seemingly "preposterous" explanation. Many of you are not comfortable in accepting that there are Beings such as "Alien Beings" or "Extraterrestrial Beings" in existence.

How then can we reach these non-believers?

> We are suggesting to your readers that Orion DRA Beings have come from a similar existence and Source to yours. Experiencing interaction with you in your form connects them with the light energy that they ultimately require. This is sounding parasitic and we understand your dilemma in trying to explain this so that it does not seem like a fantasy.

Will we learn more about their condition in subsequent Volumes?

> What you must convey in this place and space in the dissemination is that Orion DRA Beings simply do

not have the ability to regenerate themselves or grow in an unrestricted Body of Light. We will continue to explain their origin in Volumes 3 and 4.

12

Nikola Tesla

NOTE: Nikola Tesla was born in 1856 AD in modern day Croatia, but lived in New York for 60 years. He was an engineer known mainly for designing the Alternating Current (AC) Electrical System and the Tesla Coil. The Coil was part of a system that could wirelessly transmit electricity. Early Radio antennas and telegraphy used this invention.

Much has been said about Nikola Tesla's attempt to provide the world with free energy. We'd like to discuss his contributions.

> Tesla was not only defining a system for creating free energy but was also creating a bonafide experience that would allow for the ignition of time travel. Tesla's Coil and transformer of the current is the same current and new signal that you are modifying in your repaired DNA.

Can we equate the transmission from Volume 1 to the current that Tesla was creating through the Coil?

> Yes. There is a magnified response of the absorption rate of what you are calling electricity and current into your cells via the transmission from Volume 1.

What is this "current" enabling in our cells?

> This aligned sequencing registers a condition that allows for intracellular communication and the deepening and absorption of the current in the cells.

Is this what Tesla was discovering?

> The indication that he had disseminated this is contained in his writings, if you equate the

> understanding that his system is integrated in an ignition switch. The stream of energy and current propels the switch. You will understand that there is no ignition switch that needs to be created. This already exists in your Light Body assembly. The ignition switch and the circuitry is contained in your Light Being embodiment. When you maintain a voluntary disconnect state of being and continue to assemble and reassemble, you are creating this very circuit.

NOTE: The "ignition switch" is a reference to the Tesla Coil. The coil was facilitating a wireless transfer of energy. Today for example, the concept is applied to such uses as wireless transmission, computers, smart phones, x-rays, robotics and laser beams. What is being explained to us is that this "discovery" or "invention" was pointing us toward intracellular communication – the exchange of energy on a cellular level.

It sounds like "free energy" was just the natural outcome of what Nikola Tesla was really investigating.

> The understanding that free energy is what Tesla was creating is a partial truth. He was also disseminating information about your own ability to be individual generators of free energy and therefore of freeform existence. Tesla had "discovered" time travel capability and this is what instigated the attack on his personal library.

NOTE: On March 13th 1895, a fire broke out at 33-35 South 5th Ave in Manhattan. Tesla's laboratory was located on the 4th floor of this 6-story building. His invention models, notes, lab data, plans and tools were reportedly destroyed. The damage was valued at $50K.

Were all his findings destroyed?

> The process and the scientific study and writings have been absconded and not destroyed. The information is being contained in the Military Libraries in the USA. The knowledge is being used to practice for a military strategy involving machinery and vehicles that have the ability to disappear and then reappear.

It's been reported that Tesla experienced visions from as early as five years old. After his brother Dane died in a riding accident he began seeing visions of the air around him filled with "tongues of living flame". If this is true, what was he envisioning?

> Tesla's contact with the intermediary world of Lyra was made at an early linear age. He was receiving early on the understanding that light and communication through light can be assembled for the purpose of time travel. What he also realized was that Man Being has the ability to generate this experience and possesses an "ignition switch" for this change.

Was this experience the catalyst for his scientific explorations?

> He understood that his experience was not a unique experience and he wanted to prove that this was available for all. The understanding that there is a measurement in the Aether that can be simulated through experiments is also what he wanted to

show. His experimentation early on is similar to the experience when you are beginning to maintain and create a Light Body embodiment in Lyra and simultaneously existing in the linear time experience.

Are you saying that Tesla was experimenting early on even as a child?

As we have already described with you there is a condition where you are maintaining a duality of existence and this expands into many existences of being. Please refer back to our discussion of the twin siblings and the Capitoline Wolf.

To clarify, you're saying that there can be multiple forms of us at one time in the 3rd density existence and that Tesla had more than one. Is that correct?

Yes. In the 3rd density Earth plane existence you are capable of existing in more than one form or more than one Being and these Beings are also assembling their Light Body embodiment in the intermediary world of Lyra.

Is that what he discovered at Colorado Springs when he said he made a connection with outer space?

NOTE: During the year that he spent at his Colorado Springs Laboratory (1899), Tesla noticed a repeating signal being picked up by his transmitter. He believed that he was receiving signal from "Outer Space" and was widely ridiculed when he announced the discovery.

> He defined that his existence was also coexisting in another density of experience. Referring to this experience as communicating with "outer space" is a correct description for it is a communication with himself in another density of experience.

This is a little mind-bending. Were all of Tesla's breakthroughs a result of his communication with Lyra?

> We are not proposing that he was given specific scientific equation and instruction. It is more like the descriptive experience that we are sharing with you. He was disseminating in a scientific jargon and explanation in order to be able to create a patent for change. He believed that if the proof could be made through a scientific trial and experiment that this could be adopted and accepted in your civilization.

You mentioned that there is a measurement in the "Aether". What did Tesla discover about Aether?

> He understood that there is a light and a light embodiment that we are not utilizing and are connected with in the Earth plane. Tesla recognized that there are other energies and other versions and phases of energy that we can also create and absorb. This is what you are referring to as "Aether".

NOTE: In 1899 Tesla built a laboratory in Colorado Springs, Colorado. He moved to this high altitude location so he could have room for his high-voltage high-frequency experiments. Tesla wished to study the conductive nature of low-pressure air, which was part of his research into wireless transmission of electrical power. By 1900 Tesla produced artificial lightning from the station's metal mast – with the largest bolt at 135 feet long.

Can you sum up what Tesla had ultimately discovered?

> You are all light generators. This is what Tesla was creating through his scientific research and what he intended to disseminate.

What specifically was documented in the writings that the US Military absconded from Tesla?

> The findings concluded that you are limited not only in your light deprivation existence but that you are also deprived of the physical experience of creating light. You are not exposing yourselves to the correct volume and intensity of light. Most important of all, you are not able to generate luminosity in order to feed yourselves and feed others with the light.

Did Tesla voluntarily disconnect?

> Tesla has made a complete voluntary disconnect and his arrival in the 3rd density plane of existence was also as a traveler or messenger for change. He is experiencing and has experienced travel through the use of the Iridis gateway of knowledge. Those who are experiencing the Ascension Event will be immediately connecting with the information that he has left in the Earth plane density – for the instruction and reformatting of belief.

Did Tesla arrive on Earth through Iridis gateway as did Jesus and Michelangelo or did he have human parents? We are told that he was born in present day Croatia to Milutin and Duka Tesla.

> This is a question that adheres to both beliefs as there was a physical birth event and there was also a simultaneously aligned event with what you are referring to as time travel, using the gateway. There are some Beings that are choosing to come into the Earth form existence in order to disseminate, as was the experience of Nikola Tesla.

How can a Being experience a human birth and also arrive via time travel?

> There are Beings who voluntarily choose to reconnect with the 3rd density experience even though they have already corrected their belief about immortality and reincarnation. This is an example of a vehicle into the 3rd density of experience that allows for a more effective dissemination for change and it is effectively a sacrifice that this Being has made in order to disseminate new beliefs and understanding. It is a difficult path as you are aware. This pathway is available for Beings who actively choose it although it is not a desirable one.

You're saying that the Being we know as Tesla is a fully ascended Being who chose to disseminate through a reincarnation experience – simply because it's a more effective way to execute change. Is that correct?

> Yes, although this is a simplified understanding. This is a remarkable Being and situation who on one hand is voluntarily choosing to experience a

reincarnation event and on the other hand also aligned itself completely with the principles of time travel and ascension. We will return to this discussion in another Volume, as your readers require further understanding of the principles of time travel.

Will we be furthering our understanding of the Iridis gateway in another volume as well?

We must stress with you in this dialogue that Iridis does not represent a person or an event, as some of your readers understand. The letters in the name Iridis stand for a completed experience and there are principles of this division that need to be reunited. There are six ways to align yourself with this experience and six ways to exist in the shape that we will be sharing with you in another dialogue. The shape and travelling in the sphere is what we are suggesting you continue to align your beliefs in. It is this geometric shape that will allow you a portal through the world that you are assembling your belief of – as in the World beyond Lyra.

Returning to the discussion of Tesla, you said that he made a "complete voluntary disconnect". To clarify for the Reader, the complete voluntary disconnect means that we achieve the Light Body release. Is that correct?

The voluntary disconnect is the responsibility in your belief for change. When we express that an individual in the Earth plane has made a complete voluntary disconnect – as Tesla did – we are speaking of the voluntary assembly of knowledge,

> the voluntary belief in reconnection and the voluntary experience that you are the change.

The Reader is making the choice to voluntarily disconnect by absorbing this information and reassembling their beliefs.

> Yes. This is not about voluntarily signing up for a disconnect experience or making an equivalent commitment. You are already in the process for voluntary disconnect when you begin to reassemble these beliefs. You are making new alliances and you are also re-equating the assembly of your Light Being with the process of the change. If you are pausing to ask, "how do I voluntarily disconnect?" then you have not arrived at the place and space where this is occurring.

You're saying that it occurs automatically as we shift our beliefs and that we don't have to ask or tell ourselves.

> Yes. You are making the choice as you disconnect from the old paradigm. Your Earth density form is reforming in the new truth. Change is created through the energy of change and awareness.

We are self-generators. Our beliefs set the change in motion.

> This is the principle that Tesla understood. Once you have designated the reconnections of the circuitry in your awareness this will automatically occur. You do not need to worry or manage or calculate how much of the ascension understanding and reconnection you are making. You will no longer be here in form and this is how you will know that you are time traveling. You will have access to

other densities and worlds of experience. This occurs once the Light Body has been released.

Tesla, at age 86, was found dead inside his room at the New Yorker Hotel. Coronary Thrombosis was the official cause of death. What actually occurred?

> His physical form was no longer capable of containing the light.

What would someone witness if they had been present during his Light Body release?

> Those who have witnessed an ascension event have witnessed a being dematerializing from solid into a gaseous and gold light. This is similar to what you see when you are burning incense or plant matter.

If he dematerialized why did they find his body in the hotel?

> The understanding that there is a single physical form – functioning in the Earth plane – is not completely correct.

Please elaborate.

> Beings who are practicing a new understanding and belief of ascension undergo a change in the physical form, as in a growth or a growing. What you will find is that the physical form changes and expands.

What actually dissolves into a gaseous state?

> There is a sub state in your physical form and there is a secondary state. The secondary state is your

> energy moving in connection between your world and our world – you are equally coinciding in both existences. There is a temporary place for the connection into a new form while you transition and make a further disconnect, as in the time travel experience in and out of a form.

Are we to understand that while we are shifting our belief in the Earth plane, as in voluntarily disconnecting, that we are concurrently growing a new form in Lyra?

> Yes. What you are witnessing during an ascension event is the release of form, but the release of form in the intermediary world of Lyra. You also have a release of life in the Earth density plane of existence. The disconnect in both Lyra and Earth occurs simultaneously but it is the release of the Light Being from the form in Lyra that you are witnessing in the Earth plane. This is what you will see as a gaseous and glowing gold light. You are experiencing a glimpse into another world when a Light Body release is made.

This would explain why Tesla's body was found.

> These Beings who have made a voluntary disconnect and ascension event have also transformed their physical body and this is now no longer equated with a carcass or a cadaver that remains for burial or for incineration. It is the secondary state or form that can change and appear to modify into a gaseous state.

What is the purpose of concurrently building a physical body in Lyra while we exist in the Earth plane?

> This other physical body resembles the containment of your new beliefs. The physical body in Lyra is not similar to your Earth body existence, as there is not the functionality that your physical form has in the Earth plane density. The physical form that you are inquiring about is an experience and is a congregation of beliefs, a pool of belief. Once there is the correct amount of belief there is no longer the need for form.

This second physical body in Lyra is forming to contain our new beliefs.

> **Yes. You believe in your form in the Earth density and when you no longer mirror this belief in Lyra then you release the form.** Your belief in form is what must change for there is no such thing as form. There is movement and movement of belief.

Is the second physical body that we are forming in Lyra equal to what we're calling the Light Body in Volume 1?

> Yes. You are reassembling your Light Body. Your Light Body does not – ultimately – require a protective shell or a belief system that contains the light. The temporary shell only exists while you are forming a new belief of Lyra. You will release this containment and exist in freeform once you release yourself fully from the 3rd density existence. At that point you will achieve a full assembly of the Light Body.

We're reassembling our Light Body. This manifests as a physical form in Lyra while we shift our beliefs in the Earth plane. Once we completely let go of our belief in the physical existence, the Light Body is released from form in Lyra. That's when ascension occurs.

> This is accurate. The Earth plane density represents all the belief that you have that is containing the light and limiting the light. The belief in light deprivation is what is inherently structured in the Earth experience. When you release the light you are no longer being the light – you are the light. There is a difference in these beliefs and you will absorb this so that the movement of the light is what you are experiencing.

13

Déjà Vu

The discussion about two forms existing simultaneously brings to mind Déjà vu. What can you tell us about this experience?

> Déjà vu is a misplaced belief. You will need to explain the purpose of your requirement to label it "déjà vu", for this is not a correct description.

NOTE: The French term Déjà vu translates into English as 'already seen'. Déjà vu is described as recognizing a moment that you have never experienced before. Science does not yet have a definitive answer as to what causes Déjà vu.

Why is "déjà vu" an incorrect description?

> You are describing something that has already occurred, while not fully believing that it has occurred. You are approving beliefs and at the same time releasing them. This is causing you to further hold onto your incorrect beliefs.

Aren't we tuning in to another stream of consciousness during déjà vu?

> Recognizing that things have existed and patterns are being recreated is not the point of the déjà vu experience.

What is the point of déjà vu?

> It is a reconnection – not a recollection experience. For this reason, "déjà vu" is a description and term that we would like you to change.

What should we be calling this experience?

You can call it a "reconnection".

What are we reconnecting with?

> You are reconnecting with the belief that you exist in light. There is no complicated truth to this.

Has our mislabeling of the déjà vu experience created a disbelief in the light?

> This is somewhat true. Déjà vu as most of you are interpreting it, is a moment of confusion that becomes stagnant energy. You are failing to embrace the confusion and immediately move to dismiss the experience. This is unconsciously creating a negative association with the reconnection experience – or déjà vu.

How can we create a positive association with this experience?

> You must begin to accept this experience as a reconnection. Belief is modified when you make reconnections. Beliefs must continue to change in order to continue the ascension journey.

Why must beliefs change?

> You are reconnecting in stages and there are many layers of understanding. You must allow a truth to unfold and not allow it to stagnate.

We understand that Déjà vu is a reconnection but it seems to occur without our input. Why do we experience it?

> Déjà vu is a preparation for modification of your time travel experiences.

Please elaborate.

> Déjà vu is a remembrance of the fluid Light Body movement and state of being. Déjà vu is a remembrance that there are other Beings who are in a physical form and are part of your assembly. We are not speaking of your Soul Ascension Group Assembly.

What are you speaking of?

> We are speaking specifically about your re-connective state and your state of being that is including many layers of experience and awareness.

In the Tesla discussion you mentioned that we are forming a body in Lyra as we voluntarily disconnect and assemble new beliefs on Earth.

> Yes. There are multi-leveled connections of experience in your density. The modifications that are occurring are occurring so that you have enough momentum and lift to engage a connection with the next density of experience. Déjà vu is a preparation.

The Light Body that we are forming in Lyra, while still in the Earth plane existence, is living out these experiences in a fluid state before our physical body does. Is that an accurate understanding?

> This is correct. Déjà vu is preparing you before the modification or "afterlife experience", as your

> readers refer to it. Modification is a more accurate term than "afterlife". You are not going to a place "after" this "life" on Earth. You are returning to your true existence.

The common thought most of us have when we experience déjà vu is – "I've been here before". You're confirming that this is actually true.

> You are not a singular Being of Light in your density of existence and awareness. You are an interconnected Being and in your present density of experience and awareness you are a multi-level Being. You exist in more than one physical form. The understanding that déjà vu signifies that something has already occurred will be modified.

What will be the modified or new understanding of déjà vu?

> That other experiences will occur, are occurring and have occurred. You are a multi-level Being.

If people aren't choosing to assemble new beliefs or pursue any knowledge of ascension, why are they experiencing déjà vu?

> Man Being experiences déjà vu as a remembrance of the fluid Light Body form. Light cannot be fully contained or imprisoned and so these remembrances are unavoidable.

If light cannot be fully imprisoned then why are we finding it so difficult to return homeward?

The dilemma you all have is that you run from the "unexplained". Your readers must ask: **Why do I continue to dismiss this monumental "out of body" experience simply because I don't fully understand it?** This is an example of how Man Being stares a truth in the face and chooses not to see it.

Déjà vu is essentially proof that we are not our physical Earth form.

> This is only part of the truth. Déjà vu is a collection of the experiences and also of the re-connective state of awareness. Déjà vu is the momentum required in order to reassemble your Being in its complete state of reconnection before the full voluntary disconnect state.

Why isn't the déjà vu experience more effective in heightening our awareness of the disconnect state? Why is our instinct to dismiss it?

> Déjà vu as you are experiencing it, is occurring after the fact. In actuality it is occurring before and after the fact – in front of you and behind you. Your lack of understanding about your position is what you are asking about.

What do you mean when you say "our position"?

> You must learn and accept that there is no past, present or future. There is no up and down or front

and back. When you accept this then you will appreciate that the mobility and the existence and understanding is equivalent to a spiral shape. This is equivalent to a spiral re-connective state of awareness.

Please elaborate.

The spiral moving in different directions and axes of experience is a better explanation. Déjà vu as you are describing it is a linear understanding, such that this has "already happened before". The fact is that it is always happening.

Just like the spiral movement.

When you learn and accept that things are always happening and occurring you will have a better re-connective experience. The déjà vu experience will continue occurring. The linear application in your understanding is superseding the correct awareness that reconnection does not stop and start. Reconnection does not have a beginning or an end.

We tend to perceive everything in existence as having a beginning and an end. That's our thought paradigm.

The reconnection is not the beginning of the connection. It is the remembrance of your awareness of the connective state.

Is there another analogy or comparable experience that we can offer readers to help them absorb the déjà vu experience?

> When you physically look at yourselves in a mirror, for those who have the physical ability to see, this is an equivalent understanding that there is a reflection or a reflection of an experience and a state of experience. There is in fact a multitude of mirrored experiences in many different directions and axes of experience.

You're saying that the multiple-mirror experience is a better understanding of what déjà vu is representing.

> Yes. The understanding that a mirror is a one sided experience is equivalent to your linear understanding and capabilities. We are asking you to remove your linear substitution in your understanding and re-equate yourselves with the spiral. This will assist you in believing that there is a multilevel and multifaceted memory or recording, as we have explained that everything is "out there".

You're stressing that we expand our notion of identity from a single Being organism to a multi-level Being. We need to accept that our consciousness exists in many versions or forms and in many planes of existence.

> When you believe this to be a clear fact you will understand that the mirror and the one-sided flow of being is the reason why you are held captive in a physical form – as you only see one way out of your experience.

If the Reader hasn't had a déjà vu experience in years does that mean that they're not making the appropriate shifts in belief?

This is somewhat correct. Please remember however that the remembrances are unavoidable. You will all experience another jolt or remembrance that will remind you that you in fact do have the continued reconnections to make. There will be a clear difference in your next déjà vu experience.

What will the difference be?

Instead of believing that something has already happened, you will believe that something has already happened to everyone around you instead of attributing this experience solely to your own experience. It is a different level or depth of remembrance and interconnected understanding and belief.

What more is there to know about the déjà vu – or reconnection experience?

Déjà vu is equivalent to swimming and also equivalent to the understanding that sea creatures swim in a different current of experience.

Please elaborate.

As an example, the octopus has many different axes of reach and assembly and energy release. This is what you will be experiencing. The movement and the interconnections of those creatures that are found deep in the sea have a momentum as well as a release of the current. Their movement affects communication not only between other creatures in the sea and the sea depths but also affects the water envelope that surrounds their Being.

Movement is communication and energy release.

> There is an exchange of energy. The ocean is not attributed solely to the movement of the water envelope and the physical movement of the Being. There is a union and a reunion such as we are coming from the sea and returning to the sea, as in the Primordial Sea and the Sea of Understanding.

When you use the term "Primordial Sea" are you referring to Lyra?

> Yes.

We should equate how Sea Creatures move and exchange energy in the water with how Man Being exchanges energy with Lyra (the Primordial Sea). Is that correct?

> Yes. When you accept that one affects the other then you will fully understand that motion and swimming is not an individual or singular experience. It requires the intention of a Being – as in time travel and momentum – and also the receptive experience of Lyra or the Primordial Sea.

We are so singularly focused on our physical Being in the 3rd density Earth plane – unaware that we are already connected with other states of being.

> This is correct.

Lyra is the Primordial Sea. Is this what is meant by "we are all returning to the Sea"?

Yes. Please understand that "gateway" and "Primordial Sea" are also an equivalent understanding. When you understand and believe that they are one and the same you will have made significant strides toward a new understanding of being. This is also something that you will be receiving more information about.

14

Fe|Male

You mentioned in a previous dialogue that women – at a point in linear history – were already in possession of ascension knowledge. We'd like to explore some female contributions to the Repair Project.

> The semblance of female and male is not a precise understanding. There is a perceived inequality between the Beings known as men and women. In actuality the responsibility for the teaching and disseminating comes through the channel that you are equating with the "female" energy.

Do you mean to say that human females have historically been our teachers – or that the Lyra Beings we have been in contact with are female?

> When we say teachers we are not speaking of Human Beings. There is an Assembly and an assemblage of Lyra Beings who are responsible for the teaching and sharing of the knowledge. We are Beings that you would consider female in spirit but this is not an exact equation or understanding.

Are you saying that when humans establish a dialogue with Lyra that we're communicating with female-like Lyra Beings?

> We are neither male nor female. We are also not a combination or a reunification, as in a hermaphroditic assembly. We are primarily light and the light is not something that you have encountered yet. This light is a light that cannot be absorbed in your current pattern of form. Light is for communication. It is a language and a language of responsibility.

This is slightly confusing as you began by saying that the responsibility for the teaching comes through female Beings.

> We have said "female energy", not female Beings. If you would like us to simplify the explanation for your readers this would be similar to a Super Female form, as in the Light Embodiment in form. There is a fall from the original source of your Being. You are not turning into or becoming hermaphroditic in a combined male and female union.

Please elaborate.

> **We are of a semblance that resembles female but we are in fact a new spirit and a new spirit of understanding.** There is no male and female as you are aware. We are a reunification of the energies that some would consider more female in spirit than the male participation.

Will we all return to this essence or new spirit?

> Yes. The Channel is the containment of all the Sirius Beings. Through time travel you will heal the differences in the male and female understanding.

Is the gender split in the Earth density simply a program to get us to procreate and perpetuate the reincarnation cycle?

> There is an innate understanding that the union or reunion of the male and female will result in a healing or repair. This is an incorrect belief as we

> have already discussed. There are Beings who are not interested in forming relationships where procreation takes place. This is an indication of an awareness, although usually unconscious, that there is no need to procreate in order to ascend. The program that you are speaking of was in fact modified drastically with the introduction of the new hierarchies in the Christian Church. There have been significant changes in the attitudes about procreation from 263 AD forward.

Will distinguishing between male and female contributions reinforce the understanding of a gender split?

> We are recommending a correct discussion about these Beings and their contribution and an explanation that they are neither male nor female. Which historical figure would you like to explore?

We'd like to speak about the Greek poet, Sappho.

> The Being you are equating with a figure known as Sappho demonstrates an extraordinary connection and requires a significant correction.

NOTE: Sappho was born ca. 615 BC and was a female poet from the Greek Island of Lesbos. Her poems were sung to the accompaniment of the lyre and her verses described the tumultuous nature of love. All that has survived of her work is a 28-line poem and most of what we know about Sappho comes to us through the works of other authors.

Sappho was a prolific poet and is reported to have recited her poetry while playing the lyre. What was her greatest contribution to the Repair Project and mission?

> You will need to make a correction for your readers. There was a mission and an undertaking to disseminate contact with the Intermediary World of Lyra through this Being known as Sappho. The understanding that this being was a Human Being is not a correct understanding.

Someone had connected with a Lyra Being named Sappho. Is that what you're saying?

> This is a correct understanding. A philosopher made use of this information and attributed it to himself. This is a correction we would like to make with you in this dialogue.

Do Lyra Beings have names or did this philosopher assign the name Sappho?

> We do not have names that you would be able to recognize. This philosopher's use of the name "Sappho" is directly related to sapphire crystal. He asked the Being to approve of this designation. Sapphire crystal is a direct connection with what we are calling the crystalline matrix. The reveal of the crystalline matrix will be shared in your final chapters of Volume 2. "Sappho" and "Sapphire" can be considered a "code word" for how to communicate with our world.

To clarify, a philosopher established a direct communication with a Lyra Being that he named Sappho – and we've misunderstood this for millennia.

> Yes. This philosopher undertook a mission to disseminate change, much as you are undertaking in

> your Volumes. The knowledge accrued from Lyra is represented in the persona he created, known as "Sappho". Sappho represented a massive change in awareness and a cultural shift. The understanding that women were able to vocalize prominently with the participation of this Being and the contribution is also somewhat correct. This Being represents a movement and a movement to disseminate information about the Intermediary World and the ascension process experience.

For final clarification, the philosopher disseminated under the pen name Sappho and there was no actual human being named Sappho. Is that correct?

> Yes. His understanding that the Lyra Being was a female was an attempt to understand what the Being was and what the Being originated in. There is a misconception that we are female in the sense of male and female. The reason for this is that Man Being has not encountered a different kind of being, one that is neither male nor female nor a combination of the two. It would make sense to attribute the Being to a female energy or entity but this is not completely correct.

What was the name of this philosopher?

> We are speaking of the Being you know as the playwright Euripides. This individual hoarded the knowledge and created writings and a system of information with a peculiar slant and adventure but did not include the full details. This Being wanted to appropriate all the information for his own use. He

> also designed a Mystery School and a group of Beings joined him.

NOTE: Born in 480 BC, Euripides was a tragedian playwright from Salamis, Greece. He is believed to have written almost 100 plays, of which a small number have survived in their entirety. He has been labelled the "most tragic of poets" and some of his major works include Medea, Hippolytus, The Bacchae and Alcestis. Euripides often used a plot device known as "deus ex machina" – where actors playing gods were brought on stage (using a machine) to provide resolution to the plot.

Did his Mystery School survive and what do we know it as today?

> This Mystery School evolved into a later practice that you are aware of today – known as Freemasonry. This Order continues today in the spirit of seeking supposed enlightenment and truths.

What more can you tell us about Sappho and Euripides?

> The understanding that Euripides was able to create a philosophical account and a treatise about the way Mankind should behave and participate with each other is what he ventured to complete. The understanding that Sappho was a Human Being in a physical form is not a complete understanding, as there was a communication and connection with Lyra.

This was a wasted opportunity to share vital information.

This is a story about the hoarding of knowledge and the undertaking to disseminate a partial truth. As you are aware, a partial truth does not assist Beings who have no concept about the Intermediary World. You are only able to process and absorb the understanding with a complete modification of beliefs. You all require the complete story and information and tools in order to complete this process. The history of Sappho is a failed dissemination attempt.

If Sappho was a Lyra Being communicating with Euripides, why isn't Sappho dated during his time period of 480-406BC? Instead, historians have dated her existence from 615-580 BC.

Please consider the events that occurred in the linear time period attributed to Sappho. The influence of Lyra and the penetration of a new belief system coincided with the linear birth and death attributed to this supposed Human Being named Sappho. Please refer to 582 BC. This was a marker.

What was the new belief system that coincided with Sappho's given dates?

There is an achievement that has occurred in this linear timespan and period. There was a new understanding about the ability to communicate without using the tools that were in existence.

What tools are you referring to?

We are speaking about sacrifices and activities of this nature. They are not essential or needed and are not responsible. A Group and School formed from this new understanding. This group and understanding and teaching was an instruction on how to retrieve the experience of communication with the lost world of Lyra.

How did the Group disseminate this knowledge?

This school of belief established the importance of the arts especially through poetry and song. They created interest in the performing arts as a method for calling upon what observers believed as the gods. This in fact was a dissemination session. Audience members would have a unique sensation and feel that they had witnessed something of artistic merit and importance. In actuality, they had received information and code.

This timespan falls in line with the inception of the Dionysia, which was a major Athenian Festival in honor of the Greek god Dionysus. It was officially placed in the Athenian Calendar in the 6th century BC.

The Dionysia was created because of this Group and the artists involved. There was an artistic movement and a revelation that is tied in with your question about the Mystery School and teaching that had occurred in this timespan. If you refer to the art and the activity of poetry and song you will understand that this group of Beings were in direct connection with Lyra. The followers and believers of this Mystery School were also performers and artists and writers and what you refer to as actors.

Historians have dated Sappho to this period because she embodies all the artistic nous that is associated with this time period. Is that correct?

> Yes. Euripides also contributed to the understanding that these mysteries and artistic developments equated with Sappho's birth. This was a time period where a school of thought and an undertaking to release information was achieved. Euripides and other contemporary Beings such as Socrates and Pythagoras were held in a close alliance and a secret undertaking to achieve understanding about their connection with Lyra.

NOTE: Socrates, born ca. 470 BC, was a Greek Philosopher who was famously put on trial for corrupting the minds of the Athenian youths. Pythagoras is believed to have existed ca. 570-475 BC – although his timeline is inconclusive. He was a Greek Mathematician and Philosopher and is famously known for the theorem that bears his name.

Euripides would have been five years old when Pythagoras died, according to our linear historical dates.

> Your documented birthdate for the Pythagoras Being is not accurate. His birth is closer to 469 BC.

Did his contemporaries all understand that Sappho was a pen name and not a real person?

> Yes.

Euripides was known as a brilliant playwright. Is this how he preferred to disseminate?

> Euripides and the lack of disclosure is an interesting point for you to note, for this being did not share everything that he was a recipient of.

We'd like to move on and discuss the contribution of Cleopatra, Queen of Egypt. Was she also involved in the Repair Project?

> This Being was monumental in creating the dissemination in a form that could be taught in lessons through an organization you would now call a mystery school. Cleopatra was responsible for teaching and teachings. Cleopatra was responsible for preparing many Beings to be aligned for the next paradigm shift.

NOTE: Cleopatra was born ca. 69 BC in Egypt and was of Macedonian Greek lineage (Ptolemy family). She was the last active Ruler of the Ptolemaic Dynasty in Egypt. Describing her affair with Julius Caesar the historian Plutarch recounts how Cleopatra smuggled herself into the palace in a bedroll to meet the Roman Consul: "It was by this device of Cleopatra's, it is said, that Caesar was first captivated, for she showed herself to be a bold coquette".

What was her mystery school known as?

> The teachings of Cleopatra were brought into the school of the Elysian Mysteries. You must correlate this school with the other mysteries you are disseminating in Volume 2. Your Volume 2 is about the mysteries as in the Mystery Schools. These were the underground movements to share the information and experience the disconnect and ascension.

Was there any evidence left behind of her teachings and involvement in these schools?

> There is a connection between many Beings you have already discovered and her initiative in the Library of Alexandria. Cleopatra placed many works in this Library that did not become destroyed. There are books that she is indirectly responsible for creating that have now been placed in the Vatican Library Archives.

What was she trying to achieve through her relationships with Caesar and Marc Antony?

NOTE: Marc Antony served as a Roman General during Caesar's conquest of Gaul (present day France, Belgium, Luxembourg, Switzerland). He was a politician and supporter of Julius Caesar. Marc Antony and Cleopatra had an infamous love affair after Caesar's death and during his Civil War with Octavian (Rome's first Emperor).

> Cleopatra was attempting to create a New World Order. One that would adopt the same principles and teachings as you have learned Akhenaten was trying to master and uphold.

What went wrong?

> Cleopatra ultimately subjugated to Julius Caesar. These two Beings had the teachings and the knowledge yet were not prepared to share their experiences and ascension principles.

That's a dramatic shift.

Cleopatra had designated on one hand much energy to saving written works and disseminating information. Cleopatra saved and hid books that were key to keeping the understanding and beliefs available, although somewhat concealed from the public. There is a definite and significant shift in her undertaking and her allegiance to the Repair Project.

What influenced the shift specifically?

The Being you are referring to as Julius Caesar had received specific guidance and advice from an official prophet who had imparted to him an initial teaching. Caesar and Cleopatra encountered an understanding and reformatted their beliefs. They both took a turn in their loyalty such that they did not adhere to the commitment to complete the dissemination, teaching and sharing of knowledge. This is another example of knowledge that was concealed and hoarded.

A romantic relationship changed the course of our history.

Cleopatra on one hand achieved much in terms of saving the written works and dedicating herself to the undertaking. The relationship that formed between herself and Caesar allowed her to change her opinions and ideas about what was to be shared and what was to be concealed. There was a significant concealment during this linear time period and knowledge was lost at this place and space.

What became of the people who had depended on her for the teachings?

> Those who had been brought to a place who were ready for a further teaching and instruction about ascension no longer had the principles available. There was a change in the allowance and permission for Beings to encounter the written works that Cleopatra had painstakingly saved for the dissemination undertaking.

This is a tragic turn of events.

> Cleopatra was once involved in a similar undertaking to you and Dramos but changed her loyalty and ideas when she aligned with Julius Caesar.

What were the works and writings that Cleopatra fought hard to preserve?

> There are writings that you would refer to as Hermetic Texts that are currently being preserved in the Vatican Library. She preserved writings and protected written accounts of the principles of not only alchemical works and written documents pertaining to Hermeticism, but also specific instruction and accounts of Akhenaten's reign and ascension experience.

NOTE: The Hermetic texts were wisdom texts, likely derived from Hellenistic Egypt. They were written in the form of dialogues and touched on theology, astrology, philosophy and alchemy among other topics. The wisdom in these texts is generally attributed to Hermes Trismegistus – a representation of the Greek God Hermes and Egyptian God Thoth.

Did she also preserve the teachings of Nefertiti?

> There are detailed books and accounts of the Nefertiti and Akhenaten adventures and journey. There are also written accounts of encounters with the Nefertiti energy in a ritualistic setting and description.

Whose encounters with Nefertiti?

> There were others who had experienced an interaction with Nefertiti through ritual. Cleopatra had read these encounters and learned of the principles and the teachings that Akhenaten received.

Is Nefertiti still available for those who wish to receive her teachings?

> This is possible and continues to be concealed from you all. There are teachers available for those Beings who wish to make the full journey through the ascension experience. The Beings that you refer to as Ascended Masters are available to many of you in the 3rd density Earth plane experience.

It's not widely known that Nefertiti is an Ascended Master.

> Cleopatra had knowledge of the Ascended Masters and had knowledge of the way to make the connection and contact, which she shared with Julius Caesar. This was information that was further

concealed after her initial reveal of what she knew and of what she already experienced.

Was Cleopatra forced to conceal against her will by Julius Caesar?

> She chose with Julius Caesar to discontinue the dissemination due to the interest in the romantic relationship and also the political power that she would achieve. Cleopatra discontinued the project because she had succumbed to another experience and wanted to use the information for further consumption and materialistic needs.

This seems to be a common theme throughout history.
> In some cases as we have already explained, Beings become fatigued. They feel that they have absorbed as much as they need to and do not further pursue the teachings and experiences that this alignment brings. This is an aborted mission if you want a simplified description of her involvement.

What more can you tell us about Cleopatra's contribution?

> She had a specific involvement with being a curator for written works. You will learn more and reveal a new understanding about the process and the message contained in these writings.

15

The Altered State

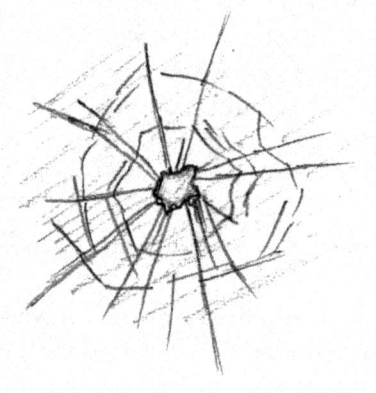

NOTE: Terence McKenna, born in 1946 was an American author and lecturer. He spoke on a variety of topics from alchemy, mysticism, technology, environmentalism and the use of psychedelics. McKenna famously described his experiences with DMT trips whereby he encountered what he called "Machine Elves" or gnomes who live in dome-shaped rooms and teach people how to create things using language.

You've said that Beings were able to encounter Nefertiti's energy through ritual. Terence McKenna described his encounters with "Machine Elves" during DMT consumption. What was he actually experiencing?

> Your understanding that there is complete awareness in an altered state during the consumption of DMT is not a complete understanding of the awareness. The breakthrough to our World is only achieved when you have a precise understanding of the World that we exist in.

Are you saying that the altered state achieves nothing unless we know what we're experiencing?

> When you are consuming DMT you are exposed to the environment but the understanding is not complete. Consumption of DMT and the activation of DMT release are two different processes and two different states of being. Consuming DMT is not giving you the assembly of the Light Body for the voluntary disconnect.

What did Terrence McKenna's drug trip experiences contribute to our understanding of the reconnective state – or Lyra?

> He disseminated to those who were believing that you can stay in 3rd density and also experience the worlds beyond. This is simply not a correct understanding. If you wish to experience the World of beyond then you must go to this World.

Did his followers and psychedelic enthusiasts believe that the "trip" itself was the World of beyond?

> His followers believed that they could experience those worlds from simply dropping and ingesting mushrooms and other plants and psychotropic medicines. This is incorrect.

The trip does spark a reconnection though – doesn't it?

> What you have are Beings travelling in a vehicle, but do not know where they are going. They are able to launch but do not understand where to land.

While tripping on DMT, McKenna described shapes that animate in front of us like "self-dribbling basketballs" – that jump into our body. He called these shapes "Machine Elves".

> Machine Elves are the components and the shapes and the building blocks of the neuro-gateway and reconnection. Your release of the Light Being occurs in stages, which can be equated with the experience of "being in shapes". This is what you can equate to the experience of the "Machine Elves".

Terence McKenna's Machine Elves are representing the Light Body Release. Is that correct?

> Yes. The understanding that the blocks or shapes are available for you is correct. The understanding that the individual blocks or shapes or "Elves" are contained outside of you is incorrect.

We are separating ourselves from what we are seeing.

> Yes. You are experiencing your inside looking outward. You are experiencing the world from within but looking from the world from without.

Why isn't this a valuable experience if we're witnessing the dynamic of the Light Body Release?

> The use of psychedelics is not necessary but more importantly you will not gain the correct knowledge or experience, as you do not understand what you are looking at or what you have immersed yourself in.

Can't users of DMT argue that this experience gets them closer to the Light Embodiment than anything else?

> This is not an effective approach. You are not experiencing the reassembly during these "trips". When you make the reassembly you will see it in the complete form, as in the Light Body – not the individual shapes or blocks or Elves. Your readers must understand that the use of psychedelics is not a recommended activity if you are seeking ascension knowledge and experience.

Why wouldn't having an elevated interaction with these shapes be of any benefit to us?

> Lyra is not a broken apart experience. The components of the primordial existence are not compartmentalized. You are speaking about a compartmentalization that occurs when someone does not have the complete experience and understanding coordinated. You are interacting in an experience without the infrastructure, preparation, modification and willingness to change. This experience does not modify you in the way that we are experiencing the modification with you in this dialogue.

This dissemination – as in the book series – is the modification that people seek through the consumption of psychotropic plants. Is that what you're saying?

> Yes. You have prepared for modification. Modification does not create a permanent understanding unless there is a permanent belief in a new understanding. Being exposed in an experience to the components of the belief does not allow for a complete re-modification of ideas and beliefs. This is too much information and experience for most Beings to process and realign. Users of psychedelics are creating a situation inadvertently where there is a further addiction experience and consumption.

The altered state experience is alluring however. It does take us out of the daily thought pattern we are all stuck in.

> Unfortunately the quest to experience the altered state of consciousness through DMT exposure or

equivalent is creating a biofeedback and addictive mechanism and state.

In our Volume 1 dialogue you said that you were "not criticizing the use psychedelics". In this Volume, you clearly are.

> Your Volume 1 reference is about gateways to heightened perception – not ascension. We do not criticize the use of psychedelics if the "simple goal" is to heighten perception. What we are suggesting is that the modification that the users of Ayahuasca or DMT are seeking is not complete. There is a glimpse or a view into the world where one reassembles the Light Body state but the Machine Elves or shapes are not able to be integrated correctly. If this were the case there would no longer be a need to repeatedly endure the Ayahuasca ceremonies or the exposure to the DMT experience.

NOTE: Ayahuasca is a brew made from the leaves of the Psychotria viridis shrub and the stalks of Banisteriopsis caapi vine (other ingredients can be added). A Shaman traditionally prepares the brew, which contains the psychedelic substance DMT. Ayahuasca has been used by Amazonian tribes for spiritual, medicinal and religious purposes.

By seeking connection through psychoactive plant consumption, we are rejecting the belief that we can self-activate.

> This is a correct understanding. The ability to generate your own equivalent experience is created in this dialogue stream as you have increased the amount of interaction with this experience, but

organically. You are able to process and create these "psychedelic" experiences by reassembling your understanding and beliefs. Exposure to DMT or other psychedelics or plants will not increase your ability to ascend. It will increase your desire to seek answers through the consumption of substances like drugs.

Using psychedelics traps us, essentially.

You are stuck at a specific channel or frequency of understanding and for some this is all that they seek in this incarnation of experience. It is not much more of an improvement to your existing status or reality, when you understand how close you are to actually utilizing these tools of understanding. This is like standing in the water and not knowing how to swim.

Some readers have reported feeling "tripped out" by the information in Volume 1. Is this confirmation that we can "organically" create the drug trip experience?

Your Volume 1 is prepared so that one needs only to read through the document and they will also experience an altered awareness. Your book dissemination – or transmission – is the "upgrade" to the pineal gland activation. The pineal activation, as you refer to it, is now obsolete. The information in your Volumes provides the altered state that Ayahuasca users are seeking. Modification will occur when one begins to ask questions as you have done in the dialogue. You will all acquire a new understanding about Lemuria and the Primordial World or intermediary state of being in Lyra.

In what way were the Ancients consuming psychedelics? We read that they used Opium, Blue Lotus Plant and that the Biblical Israelites ate Manna, for example.

> The Ancients acquired the ability to connect and integrate themselves with the plant magic and healing so that the plant energy and being became a synergy. It is this synergistic alliance that you are misinterpreting. You must realign how you regard the plant world so that a cooperative alliance is created. Plants are not here to be "used". They are not here for your benefit – they are here for your realignment. When you realign with the energy and the teaching, you will be further ahead.

How exactly did the Ancients integrate themselves with "plant magic and energy"? Did they consume them or not?

> You have all misunderstood what the Ancients achieved with the plant world. They understood the synergy between your energies.

To clarify – the Ancients weren't achieving reconnection by consuming psychedelic plants. They were simply aligning their frequency with that of the plant world.

> The Ancients had this knowledge. References to them ingesting psychedelic material is more a reference to them becoming like the plant. It is this consciousness that must be absorbed or "consumed" and not the plant itself.

We believe that the Ancients were sitting around a campfire getting high. They were simply reconnecting with plant consciousness.

> Yes. You are all being asked to be regenerative in your ability – as the plant is. In the way that you believe plants grow, so will your Light Body. You are being asked to reassemble your Being and existence.

We are externalizing the healing when we consume DMT and psychedelics.

> You are learning what the plant consciousness is about. It is best to learn what it is about and honor the process instead of becoming reliant on an outside source for reconnection. Your "healing" is from within. When we say "from within" we are referring to the Light Body as opposed to treating the form. Many of you have experienced a reconnected state though psychedelic ingestion – but are still blind.

Those who consume psychedelic plants might argue that they simply want to experience "another world" or "state of mind"?

> What many of you are undertaking is a start and stop experience. There is a release and an experience but there is also the return to the original state of being.

Users of psychedelics would argue that the impact is everlasting.

> These individuals may feel "changed", but are they ascending? They are not. Many of your readers have eagerly anticipated a discussion on the use of psychedelic plants – because they are quietly aware

of its shortcomings. We are only confirming what many of you already know.

Why then do psychotropic plants exist?

Why some plants have psychotropic or psychedelic properties is an interesting discussion. Plants and trees are in place in your world of existence so that you can cooperate with the energies and continue your travel through the gateway of experience. Your understanding that plants are here for a sacred purpose is correct. This is the main reason why the diet of the plant is encouraged, as there are many avenues to obtain information. Information is collected through the absorption of plant material.

Can we collect information from absorption of animal or insect Beings?

This is not a correct use or interaction between these Beings. We will discuss your connection to animals in another dialogue. Plants have an ability to help with the ascension process and experience. Plants are the fuel of ascension and those who are mandating the vegetarian or the vegan lifestyle are closer to "eating with God".

Are you advocating that we stop eating animals?

We are not advocating that you promote a vegetarian or vegan or raw food diet. We are advocating the understanding and the respect for what you are calling the plant world and the plant state of being.

Is that why Moses is quoted saying that "Manna" is "the bread that God has given you to eat"?

> There is good reason why this allegory and the understanding of the Tree are figured prominently in the Bible, specifically in the Genesis work. It is not only to honour the Primordial Being that you are referring to as The Channel but also to explain the plant and the plant energy.

Are they a similar energy?

> Yes. The allegory of "Mother Nature" is also where this stems from. Please remember that even using the word "stem" comes from plant symbolism. Everything is created from the plant symbolism and the plant state. You will soon look at your volume of dissemination quite differently and point out sections that do in fact refer to plants or the plant state of being.

Is plant life the passageway to Immortality?

> Plant is an existence and an exchange of energy. There is much communication that is going on through the plant world that Man Being is ignoring. All the information is around you. You do not necessarily need to eat or digest in order to communicate and absorb.

Is this why adolescent humans have made drug use a rite of passage – is there an innate attraction to consuming plants?

> The need to embrace the plant world on a deeper state or a deeper allowance of being is what you are

inquiring about. There is a need to consummate a deep connection with the plant world and Man Being has forgotten how to achieve this.

It seems that we have neglected that we are surrounded by plant life on this planet.

Your atmosphere and your existence is primarily plant and when you accept this understanding you will begin to look at the world differently. You will exist as though you are swimming through a forest or experience of a forest. The plant world is what is holding you together as Beings who are containing the information to exist in the World of Immortality.

What do you mean when you say that the plant world is holding us together?

Without the plant information or support in the infrastructure you will not exist. This is not a condition where we are saying that you need more plants to create more oxygen for better air quality. There is a mesh and a network that is designed for you to navigate through to the next world.

Please elaborate on that point.

If you regard the interconnection and intercommunication in the plant world as your medium for existence and movement you will be further along in your understanding. You can actually swim through the sea of the plant world existence and this will create a passage to the Intermediary World of Lyra. The plant world is your true "atmosphere".

How can we improve our communication with the plant world?

> Your readers are in direct communication with the plant world in this Volume 2 dissemination experience. You will all be experiencing a closer alliance and communication with the plants in the 3rd density Earth plane existence. You will be able to achieve further understanding without having to consume or smoke or inject or drink the information. The information is part of you and is all around you.

We've discussed vegetarianism, veganism, raw diet and the consumption of psychoactive plants. The youth group that we are now calling the "Millennial" generation appears to be attuned to the aforementioned practices. Are they ushering in the New Age?

> They are aware unlike no other Being who has recently existed in the Earth plane density. The Millennial Beings understand that there is another world.

Most non-Millennial readers would argue that the opposite is true – that Millennials are generally more detached from Mother Nature than any other group in history.

> They are tapped into a direct line of experience but are fettered and obstructed with the sonic sea of interference and cell phone obstruction. On one hand they are directly connected with the source of the solution and on the other hand they are creating all the problems.

Will Millennials absorb this information quicker than others?

> Millennials are interested in learning not only about themselves but how they interconnect with the universe. Their contact with what you are calling Machine Elves is a question that they would most undoubtedly like to have answered. They are aware that there is something going on but are not aware how to correctly use the information.

Why did Baby Boomers gravitate to psychedelics in the 60s?

> The push toward drugs and psychedelics is a push for ascension. When people join and commit to ascension without the preparation, these are the avenues that one seeks. This can be said of all the other addictions, be it drugs or alcohol or shopping or food or sex.

How are food and shopping addictions connected to ascension?

> What we are saying is that without a full understanding of ascension, these are avenues to attempt to change your state of being. The dissatisfaction for the status quo and the need to release yourselves and make a change is what you are inquiring about. It is very easy to temporarily alter your state of awareness. This does not however equal ascension or ascension effort. What we are trying to achieve with you is a permanent reassembly. The altered state that you all seek must become a permanent state of being. Currently your altered states are merely inebriated states.

Why are we still trapped in the Earth plane if we're enveloped by plant world information?

> You have receptors in your Being that are able to correlate and connect with the frequency of plant communication. These receptors as in your DNA structure, are aligned with the plant energy but are not completely functioning when you are entering a physical form.

Will the modification and repair to the DNA allow us to reconnect with the plant consciousness?

> You do not have the capability to repair your own DNA if you do not have the belief in the repair of the DNA. It is the belief system and the modification in your belief that you can repair your own DNA that will connect you with the plant experience.

Are there currently Beings on Earth who demonstrate this ability?

> Yes. Those Beings who are aligned with plant communication are also Beings that you equate with the Shaman or the Shamanic state and ability. These Beings have fully activated their DNA repair sites and are able to communicate with plant and what you call nature. Be aware however that those Beings who are teaching others through ingestion of activities like the Ayahuasca mixture are not as well intentioned as you believe them to be. The understanding that by consuming Ayahuasca you will achieve visions of the correct alignment is not a correct belief. Much of the Ayahuasca practice and

experience has become a commercial activity and another consumer or consumptive practice.

What more can you tell us about the use of psychedelics?

You must believe that you have the ability for unlimited growth, as a plant does. Plants are not contained in the construct of form that you believe you are. Your form is stagnant, whereas the form of the plant is ever changing. There is a constant exchange of cellular information between Man Being and the plant world. The form that you are creating in Lyra is similar to the form that you are experiencing with the plants in 3rd density. The Ancients had the ability and knowledge to integrate the understanding and awareness that plants are not in the 3rd density by accident. They are growing into your world and are enveloping you. The plant world is here to help you create a new form that allows you to exist in light.

Some readers will be disappointed that we aren't endorsing the use of psychedelics.

We appreciate that this explanation is not intriguing enough for your readers in Volume 2. You are asking "why can't readers take psychedelic plant drugs if they are reconnected with the truth?" The answer is simple: There is no restriction on taking plant medicine, but once you have connected with the medicine it no longer increases your ability to ascend or reconnect. It is a single reconnection. It is a singular moment and experience. Please appreciate that the psychedelic "trip" is simply a one off experience.

16

Persephone and Demeter

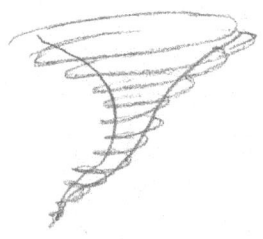

NOTE: In Greek Mythology, Persephone is the daughter of Demeter, Queen of the Harvest. Hades, god of the Underworld, falls in love with Persephone and abducts her. He claims her as his wife in the Underworld, leaving Demeter aggrieved and the Earth barren by consequence. Zeus orders Hades to return Persephone to Demeter so that the crops can grow once again. Persephone returns to Earth during the spring but having eaten the fruit of his world, a pomegranate, she must rejoin Hades come winter.

Would an examination of the Persephone & Demeter myth shed more light on plant consciousness?

> The Persephone and Demeter allegory is connected to the realm that you are creating in the New World beyond Lyra. The decision to integrate this experience is one that we will speak upon now.

What is this allegory explaining?

> If you consider "time" as a whirling motion, much like a tornado, there are openings that are created in this event. The creation and existence of these pockets of place – or portals – is what the Persephone myth is describing.

Are you suggesting that Persephone's shift into the Underworld is representing our shift in beliefs? Does the Underworld represent an "opening" from which we can shift awareness?

> This is correct, but a preliminary understanding.

What does the Reader need to absorb from this myth?

> The understanding that there are instantaneous openings such that you can redefine your belief by redefining the space is what you need to absorb. This is a question of place and space and when you have place, you create space. This is akin to what was – purportedly – taught by the Jesus Being.

What teaching are you referring to?

> "Ask and it will be given to you. Seek and you will find. Knock and the door will be opened to you".

NOTE: The above passage is found in the New Testament Book of Matthew, Chapter 7 verse 7.

Why do you say "purportedly" – are you suggesting that Jesus never uttered that phrase?

> This is an idea that was created in the Bible story so that you can reestablish your placement in the universe. This phrase or idea is a unique understanding that space and place equates with awareness and awareness equates with assembled and reassembled beliefs.

By asking or seeking, we create an opening. That opening is the gateway for time travel and existing in freeform.

> This is correct. There is an opening now in your reconnection so that you can expand your awareness, as in expanding your reach through different vibrations and frequencies.

When you refer to a plane of existence as a "density" (e.g. 3rd density), are you describing the level of vibration and frequency?

> As we have already mentioned, density is the availability and speed of light that you are able to absorb. Density is also a level that is moving in and out of what you are referring to as a time gradient.

The Persephone and Demeter myth is about time and time travel. Is that correct?

> The Demeter and Persephone mythology is about reaching through to the connective and reconnective awareness – or Lyra – such that you are integrating all the levels of awareness in the collective stream.

By creating space to expand our awareness, we are moving through the time gradients – we are learning to time travel.

> Yes. When you ask, "how do I time travel", the Persephone myth is the explanation. You will be able to move time once you absorb the understanding of this story.

What precisely do Hades and the Underworld represent in this myth?

> They represent the origin of your truth and the destiny that you encounter when you reabsorb the understanding about the immortal existence. The "Underworld", as you are referring to it, represents the repressed understanding and it also represents the danger in revealing these truths, as the reveal of

a concealed understanding is always met with controversy.

Does this mean that Hades is initiating Persephone by kidnapping her?

> Yes. Hades is readjusting Persephone's belief, as in the belief that is destroying Man Being. You can reabsorb a "new" understanding when you discontinue the hijack of the truth.

This tale is somewhat confusing in that Hades' kidnapping of Persephone would imply that he is taking her against her will.

> This is a kidnapping so that the beliefs can be readjusted and new understandings can be reconnected and absorbed.

Hades is actually saving her.

> The direction is such that she is being saved from Mankind, as the belief in the undertaking does not exist in the Earth plane. It exists in a concealed awareness, which is represented by the Underworld. It exists in between the light and the experience of the belief follows the experience in the belief.

Hades' three-headed dog Cerberus guards the gateway to the Underworld and ensures that the dead never leave. What does Cerberus represent?

> You are asking about a gatekeeper and a gatekeeper as in concealed knowledge. Please consider that the figures and allegories and archetypes that seem to be from another world are in fact concealed

> knowledge. These are often figures that you perceive as threatening or scary and for this reason concealments are not being brought to the forefront. That which Man Being has become terrified of is the knowledge that he actually seeks.

Yes. You've made this point before.

> This is something that you are correcting in your dissemination. These 3rd density constructs bind you in unnecessary fear and anxiety about who you are and what is the best path to choose. Fears and these concepts and ideas that terrify you are in fact gatekeepers and markers for things that are necessary to rework and reexamine. The fables and allegories that have been disseminated throughout your existence continue to weigh you down. You continue to question why these stories exist and why there is no other way of regarding them.

Will our discussions about misinterpreted myths exhaust the readers?

> You are turning many of these stories upside down and inside out. There may be a question or a criticism that you are reshaping and reinventing everything that you come across or meet. This is however part of the Repair Project, as much of what has been disseminated throughout your linear history has been reorganized and shaped into unnecessary beliefs. The concept of disbelief is also what you must reassemble for your reader.

Why does Cerberus have three heads?

> The concept of the three headed dog is similar to the three levels of experience in the disconnect. That is what is being concealed in this construct. There is a place where you must shift out of form and redesign and believe in a new identity so that your form can be reassembled as you time travel.

Can we equate Cerberus with the Wolf mythology and the belief in shape shifting?

> This is a tale connected to Sirius and the Dog Star analogy. The dog or the wolf symbolism – as attributed to the connection with Sirius – is what has been twisted and misshapen beyond all recognition. The three headed dog is defining the disconnect experience in three stages. This is a tale about the ability to disconnect and move in and out of form. This has now become a terrifying monstrosity of a creature so that you dare not even explore a curiosity in the voluntary disconnect principle. The idea of a ravenous beast who guards your passage only creates anxiety and terror in the common psyche of Man Being and the "collective unconscious" as you refer to it. You are being terrified away from the concepts of existing free of form.

We have been programmed to fear our "salvation".

> You must understand and relay the following to your readers. Many of the things that go "bump in the night" as your pop culture describes, are the very things that will help you to remove yourselves from the imprisoned state. **The things that**

you are terrified of or never experience are the things that you need to face in order to reassemble a new belief.

Cerberus allows Persephone's return to Demeter, which ushers in the spring season. What is being conveyed through this event?

> Persephone is making the journey homeward after having reawakened the belief. You will all, like Persephone, rise again and become one with the World of Immortality.

Why does Demeter grieve Persephone's kidnapping if her daughter is absorbing the truth about her existence?

> When Persephone returns to "Earth", this is symbolic of her return to Lyra and the reconnective state. She is not in actuality returning to the 3rd density Earth plane. When you ask, "Why is Demeter grieving the loss of Persephone?" this is a misunderstanding. She is not grieving the loss of her daughter – she is grieving for the rest of you who have not yet taken the journey homeward, as Persephone has.

Persephone has shown us how to make the journey. Can we equate Persephone with the Sirius Beings that are waiting in Lyra?

> Yes. Persephone can be equated with the Beings that have already made the disconnect. They are waiting for the Soul Ascension Group to return – en

masse – so that you can all journey homeward to your World of Origin.

To clarify, even if we have successfully disconnected and released our Light Body, we must wait in Lyra for everyone else to ascend.

> Yes. When you make the voluntary disconnect you are still awaiting the rest of the Soul Ascension Group to make the complete transition and time travel experience. Persephone symbolizes a key. The Persephone and Demeter myth describes the experience of maneuvering in between the worlds and in between the light.

To summarize, Persephone's marriage to Hades is an initiation of the truth. She has been made aware and has disconnected.

> This is correct.

We are the Beings who must make our way back, just as Persephone has.

> This is an accurate understanding. Your readers must take the journey to the "Underworld" and rediscover the concealed truths. You are providing the "Underworld" experience with your book dissemination.

You're associating the Underworld with concealed truths. What does this say about blackness or darkness?

> Darkness represents light energy. The deepest black shines a light and this is what Persephone

represents. This is why both of your visions of The Channel describe the deepest black.

Darkness coincides with the truth of our existence.

> This is correct. Persephone makes the journey to reconnect and therefore voluntarily disconnects.

When Persephone is kidnapped, Demeter is overcome by grief and changes her form to an elderly woman. What does this represent?

> Demeter's transformation represents your inability to make the time travel and connection. It represents your containment in the Earth plane. Aging is an allegory and represents the involuntary death construct.

This particular device is representing how we are trapped and must reassemble in the Soul Ascension Group.

> This is a correct understanding. Demeter's search is representing your search for the reconnection. Demeter's presence as an elderly woman symbolizes your imprisoned state and paradigm of beliefs. Your readers must understand that in the World to come, there is no aging. It is a timeless existence in the Immortal state. Time travel is the Immortal state of being.

While Demeter grieves the Earth goes barren. What does this represent?

> The Earth goes barren as a representation of being locked out of the World of Immortality.

We'd like to address the episode within the myth whereby Demeter is invited to be the nursemaid for Queen Metanaira's newborn son in Eleusis (a Greek town 12 miles northwest of Athens).

NOTE: Demeter, in disguise as an elderly woman named Doso, is hired to nurse the Queen's infant son. Demeter anoints him with ambrosia (food of the Gods) and begins to transform him into a divine Being. Each night, Demeter dangles the baby over a fire to help him achieve an immortal state. When the Queen spies on her and witnesses the ritual, she screams in horror. Demeter drops the infant and reacts in anger. She chastises the Queen for interrupting the ritual and ruining the baby's chances at immortality.

Why does Demeter hold the baby boy over the fire?

> The holding of the baby over the fire is equivalent to the disconnect experience and also the experience of being in front of The Channel or Medusa. This can also be equated with being in front of the "burning bush", as was presented in your Bible. The fire is representing the "afterlife" or immortal state.

What is the importance of the baby being a boy?

> You are being reminded of the misinterpretation of the warrior narrative. The boy is representing your warrior heroes.

Are you referring to Perseus?

> Yes, and to all warriors who go forth and find their way in the afterlife and arrive as a hero when they return.

We've falsely believed that Perseus is a hero because he slays the Medusa. Demeter is demonstrating that the boy must become one with the fire and not "survive" it. Is that correct?

> Yes. Please understand that the Perseus myth and the slaying of Medusa represent the cutting off of the gateway or connection. This story of Persephone and Demeter is rebuilding the gateway and the connections. The nursemaid episode is explaining how to rebuild the connections with Lyra and the World beyond.

Demeter does not complete the anointing of the baby. Why not?

> The baby is denied the achievement of the immortal state. The punishment on the baby is equivalent to punishment on Man Being. The baby's Mother represents the choice Man Being continues to make whereby you sever the connection. The boy represents the severing of the connection with the afterlife.

Demeter orders the Queen to build a Temple to her in Eleusis as penance for her distrust. What does this symbolize?

> This is a call to redirect the belief system toward the female or divine feminine and what is represented by the plant world. This world is not specifically a world filled with plant life. The energy from which the plants are drawing their sustenance is what you are calling the plant world. This is a tale to redefine your beliefs and remember that there is something beyond the Earth plane and also beyond Lyra. Many of you have already obtained a profound connection with the Intermediary World but are not

able to move beyond Lyra, as you do not yet have knowledge of The Channel.

When Persephone eats the Pomegranate in the Underworld this allows Hades to claim her for half the year. Can we draw a parallel to Eve eating the apple from the Tree of Knowledge?

> The Tree of Knowledge is presented as something that is not within your reach. This is to understand that it is not knowledge that you should or can accumulate. You should accumulate experience. The downfall of Man Being occurred when you shifted away from a belief in experience.

The Eleusinian Mysteries were annual rites practiced in honor of Persephone and Demeter. Why is the Greek town Eleusis important and why are the mysteries named after this town?

> This represents a geographical location where a large group of Beings accepted this teaching and belief en masse. What occurred in your linear historical accounts was a redirect in the belief of form so that many paradigms collapsed and many Beings left. This may look like there was an abandonment of this city or town but in fact this is not correct, as many made the journey homeward.

You are speaking of a mass Ascension Event.

> Yes.

17

The Elysian Field

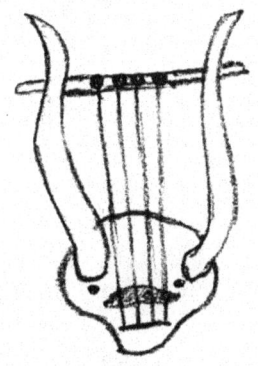

The town of Eleusis was once a gathering place for ascending Beings and the assembly of knowledge. Modern day Eleusis does not attract the same attention. Why is that?

> There were many who made the ascension experience through the voluntary disconnect. The energy was taken with the Beings that made a disconnect. Recall the concept of cutting through time as in a whirlwind or a whirl of energy. This is what occurred.

Does this mean that an Ascension Event leaves destruction in its wake?

> Please understand that when ascension occurs en masse there is a monumental change in the energy and frequency experienced by those Beings who remain behind. Beings who do not wish to pursue their own ascension experience will be experiencing a sickness and discontent on a large scale as in a malaise or in a cultural revolution. We are not speaking of a positive revolution.

What specifically occurs after a mass Ascension Event?

> There is always an experience for those Beings left behind whether it is in your atmosphere, or geographically or geologically or socially or financially. There are many levels of experience that may not be beneficial for those Beings left behind. The need and the requirement to reshape the belief system is not an option after a mass Ascension Event, as many things will be imploding and no longer exist. The Notre Dame event is simply a small example of what is to come.

There is a massive project to clear out shipwrecks in the area around Eleusis. Why are so many ships being abandoned in this location?

NOTE: The Eleusis Port Authority has identified 52 wrecks, which need to be removed from the gulf area. Many of these sunken or half sunken ships have been abandoned and pose an environmental risk, as a number of them are still leaking fuel into the water.

> In this geographical region there continues to be an effort to disseminate the practice of the voluntary disconnect through the continued understanding of the Mystery School. Many are still striving to achieve the Elysian Field state, which is very much the same as the Lemuria state.

How is this affecting the ships?

> This new current of understanding is transforming the physical plane such that movement on the water or through the air has become less predictable and more of a challenge. There will continue to be accidents and activities where vehicles are no longer able to stay on course as per their radar measurements. This is a definition that the portal or the gateway for the mass ascension experience is being used.

There have been other mass ascension experiences. Does that mean that there are other "portals" in different locations?

> Many areas on your planet in your 3rd density experience have these situations existing where there is an imbalance due to a hole or a tear remaining

after a mass ascension event. This is the disconnect experience and the result of the energy shift and the cut through time.

Can anyone access these holes or portals?

These portals are not accessible for the Beings who remain behind. This portal of experience is aligned with those Beings who are part of the same Repair Project.

The Beings left behind will soon create their own portals, as you've said.

The Beings that remain behind will experience much difficulty and much effort will be needed for these Beings to ascend. They will however recreate their own portal and gateway with their own experience and knowledge of experience.

In what linear year did this mass ascension happen at Eleusis?

There is a pivotal understanding in the year 600 BC. This is a linear time period where an event changed the belief system and ascension began to occur en masse. This was shortly disrupted thereafter and from approximately 492 BC to approximately 343 BC there was a deficiency, as the activity ceased. After these linear time periods there were changes again, as the beliefs surrounding the voluntary disconnect were once again disseminated. There has been a prevalence of the teaching and understanding in this area that you are defining as Greece.

NOTE: In 600 BC, the Eleusinian mysteries become part of the official Athenian religious calendar. The Persians destroyed Eleusis in 479 BC but Pericles begins a rebuilding program ca. 450 BC. In 360 BC Eleusis is again expanded and fortified.

We'd like to disseminate further understanding of the Eleusinian mysteries. What more can we know about this experience?

> Your readers will want the instructions on how to achieve the experience, as you now have an understanding that there is a world beyond Lyra. You are being invited to explore this experience further with our instruction and guidance. You must however master the principles that you are developing on your own.

NOTE: The Eleusinian mysteries were annual rites performed by ancient Greeks at the town of Eleusis. The mysteries were a symbolic retelling of the Persephone and Demeter myth and initiates were sworn to secrecy. The historian Plutarch was a participant of the Eleusinian mysteries, as noted in a letter he wrote to his wife after the death of their daughter: "because of those sacred and faithful promises given in the mysteries…we hold it firmly for an undoubted truth that our soul is incorruptible and immortal".

Are you referring to the "Man Being" dissemination when you say to "master the principles that we are developing on our own"?

> Your written dissemination as in the "Man Being" books are the passport to this next world of experience and beyond. Through this gateway is the

immortal experience that you are explaining as time travel. The books and your understanding through the upcoming volumes will present the findings that you are achieving of your own merit and absorption.

Are all the tools being presented in our book dissemination or does the Reader need to engage in a supplementary activity?

Your readers and those Beings who are equated with the Sirius experience will want this instruction, as you already understand this to be true. Your Man Being book dissemination is the instruction required for the reconnection.

To clarify, there aren't any supplementary activities the readers can partake in to achieve further reconnection. Is that correct?

The "activity" your readers will partake in is the sharing of the knowledge. You are a Soul Assembly Group and the sharing of the knowledge is a key component of your ascension journey.

This is not an easy book to share for some.

This is not a correct understanding. Your readership will be sharing the Volumes publically as they now understand their responsibility in the Repair Project. Beings who do not wish to share the information are not of Sirius origin. Many of your readers will turn to their social media platforms to speak about the book. This will lead to an acceleration of the project.

Will Volume 2 complete the Reader's initial reconnection process?

> Yes. Your readers will have completed the reconnective awareness and will be able to function in a reconnected state of awareness. This will form the desire to eliminate those things that you are equating with Earthly constructs.

Dramos and I cannot completely withdraw from our 3rd density constructs – yet.

> This is not a requirement to destroy and deconstruct your 3rd density experience, as you must still bring those remaining Sirius Beings to a collective awareness. Your connection with the Earth density is a responsibility that you are upholding and this is the reason why you are both trapped, as you have committed to this undertaking before in previous incarnations and did not make a successful completion. You are dedicated in this incarnation of experience to complete the transition and complete the transmission in the disseminated works.

We have made the decision to return and disseminate information.

> You were both prevented from disseminating information in previous incarnations. You are not blocked or stopped in this experience of incarnation and your Volumes will be disseminated and read.

Before we conclude this discussion, we'd like to examine the Elysian Field state and what the Eleusinian mysteries were revealing.

> Please refer to the painting titled "Elysian Fields" by the artist known as Carlos Schwabe. This is a very strong symbol and also a guidance for your readership. The expression in this painting is a suitable benchmark for how much information you can share in Volume 2.

NOTE: Carlos Schwabe was a Swiss painter born in 1866. He was a Symbolist painter whose pieces often depicted a dreamlike universe. Symbolist art was a counter movement to realism and Schwabe embraced the fantastical elements of mythology and biblical allegory.

Are you referring to information about the Elysian Field state or the Mysteries?

> The understanding that the plant world is a gateway of understanding is something that your readers will need to absorb. They do not need to absorb the full mystery at this place and space. You can begin to suggest that there is an absorbable understanding about the world of plants and nature. The divine female energy, as you refer to it, is waiting for your readers in this construct. The painting is a suitable mystery and this is a level of understanding that will be absorbed in Volume 2. You will want your readers to continue their journey and the pacing of the dissemination is key.

Why is pacing the dissemination so important?

> If there is a burdening of too much information and codes released, you will lose many in their inability to reformat their beliefs. You are proceeding at the correct pace.

MAN BEING

This painting is a starting point for a renewed understanding of the Elysian Field state. Is that correct?

> This is an ideal example of what you will need and want to convey to your readers. The way to explain to the Reader is fulfilled in this painting and in this constructed idea about the World to come. The mystery is the first step through the gateway into the field of experience and into the field of the plant knowledge.

Some readers who partake in psychedelic plant consumption might interpret the "Elysian field state" as a drug high.

> This is not correct. Please choose carefully how you wish to express the plant knowledge so that you do not push your readers into the belief that they must ingest drugs in order to experience this belief. This is what you will be correcting through Volume 2.

You want us to make clear that the use of psychedelic plants is unnecessary.

> You can experience this gateway without consuming material in plant form. This is a key concept in Volume 2 that will help you assemble the Group that you have taken responsibility for in the homeward journey. Please direct your focus toward the painting now.

What do we need to know about the artist, Carlos Schwabe?

> This Being has made a voluntary disconnect experience. The artwork that this Being has generated in this linear time period is very much

representational of his desire to return homeward. The allusion that this is achievable is very believable. This Being has made the disconnect and the journey. This is the story of the path of the lyre and the world beyond. The paintings that were created in the later years of Schwabe's physical existence are ones that you can look at and examine further.

NOTE: We recommend that you observe the painting while the Lyra Beings deconstruct the meaning. Search: "Elysian Fields Carlos Schwabe". It depicts a woman in a green dress holding a lyre.

Who is the woman being depicted in his "Elysian Fields" painting?

> This is an amalgamation of a woman that this artist was involved with romantically and also the archetype of the divine feminine and the Demeter mystery that you are beginning to explore.

The woman is holding a lyre. She is also pointing to her heart, which is radiating light. Please explain the symbolism.

> The lyre is trailing behind her, indicating from where she has arrived – through the Intermediary World of Lyra. The light that is emanating from her chest is an indication that the light is not contained or trapped, as you have previously experienced in your Earth plane. The light moves and the light is released and the light continues to move. The light is not contained in form or held in form.

She is pointing to her chest to indicate that we are of light. Is that all?

> The hand at the chest pointing to the light is signalling to look at the light and not hide from the light, as what has been taught and conditioned with those followers of the Abrahamic religions.

What specifically were followers of the Abrahamic religions taught?

> They are told to look away from the light while "alive" and then to go to the light in the involuntary death experience. This is an unfortunate belief, as they need to look at and embrace the light before this experience.

What else is represented through this painting?

> The painting is telling viewers that you are becoming one with the plant world. **You are now in between the light and in between the light there exists the knowledge of travel and immortality.**

What do you mean by "we are in between the light"?

> The light has many levels. Instead of looking at the light you are becoming light and this is also suggested in this painting. You are looking at what you become. The attire of the woman in the painting is a blend of the field and what lies beyond. You are becoming one with this field and when you

understand what the field is you will proceed and have completed your final Volume.

Are the flowers in the painting of a specific genus?

> These flowers allow one to fall asleep, as in the Valerian plant for example. They contain a chemical that allows one to sleep. It represents the dream state and the elixir that Man Being believes must be consumed as in a drink. In actuality the elixir must be absorbed as in the light.

Why is the lyre a symbol for ascension and Lyra?

> The understanding that an instrument is what is played to make a connection with the world of Lyra is something that has been created as an allegory or an archetype of experience. The definition of the use of the instrument is to create a frequency and an experience.

Are you saying that the reconnection with Lyra requires a hearing experience – as in attuning to sound frequency?

> The creation of a physical instrument symbolizes the achievement of the reconnection. The truth is that you will no longer need to speak using a physical speech. This is what is mostly represented in this instrument. The sound of the light when you reconnect and reassemble your beliefs is a peculiar sound that you will all be generating. Your physical voices and spoken words will be changing as you continue this experience.

We have noticed that our vocal cords feel exhausted more often. Is this an indication of what you are describing as a transition to non-verbal communication?

> You have already made an observation that you are experiencing a change in the sensation of your throat area. This is a correct understanding and is not a consequence of physical speaking and exhausting the vocal cords. This is an understanding that the vocal cords will now be changing position and the vibration in the spoken sound that you attempt to make will now have a new sound.

What is that sound like?

> The sound is similar to the quality of a string instrument and the lyre. The world of Lyra will be revealed to you in a further dialogue, as this is an important understanding that you will want to share. For now, understand that the sounds that you make and generate will have a new quality. As you begin to absorb further Volumes, you will recognize that in fact the physicality of speaking will soon feel different to you all.

What will we be experiencing?

> You will be noticing and explaining that there is an extreme vibration in the throat area and you feel that you are generating a sound without using much inhalation or expiration. The sound is resonating in your Light Being and generating a noise that is further signalling to others to approach. You will be attracting other Beings to the project from the frequency that you are emitting.

Is this is all occurring on an unconscious level?

> You are not aware of what is happening, as you do not have the capacity to hear this frequency in this place and space. Other Beings are aware of your capacity to generate this frequency and sound. You will be attracting the attention of other Beings, both Human and animal and you will notice a new connection and a collaboration with them.

18

The Plant World

We'd like to speak directly on the topic of plant world consciousness.

> Plant consciousness, as you are referring to this experience, is equivalent to a new level or understanding of energetic connections. Plants are not here for your benefit. They are here for your realignment. There is a precise definition and a difference in this equation.

Please elaborate on the difference.

> Plants do not simply represent a new understanding or awareness. They are representing your new condition. You are not becoming a plant. You are in fact of this dimension.

Are you saying that plant is a dimension of experience?

> This is a correct understanding.

Are plants from of our world of origin – have we taken plant consciousness into the 3rd density with us?

> When you reconnect with plant life you will see an experience that belies the truth about your origin and your state of being.

What can we learn from the plant state of being?

> Please envision the leaf from a plant and a vein in its membrane structure. As the idea comes in, the repair and processing permeates out in all different directions.

The plant structure is demonstrating how we should process information. Is that correct?

> Yes. You must allow the processing of your understanding to create a field just as liquid is travelling through the membrane and vein system of a plant leaf.

We need to allow our belief streams to flow in infinite directions – the way a plant absorbs water and grows.

> Precisely. Put simply, we are speaking to you about the expansion of what you call consciousness. You are maintaining a level of consciousness in the Earth plane that is equivalent to a straight line and an exacting process. This has no benefit, as it cannot build upon new connections.

Plants are showing us how to exist.

> As a plant grows in different directions so will all of you in this discussion. The process where you allow the feeling and the absorption to permeate in different directions is the process that you are relearning. There is a history of plant research and interest in discovering why plants grow a certain way and it is this understanding that will benefit you all.

What are researchers discovering?

> The understanding that as a fern frond unfolds there is a transmutation and awareness is something that is commonplace in your lexicon. However, you do not yet understand that your own cells can adjust

and group themselves. This adjustment enables you to learn and absorb in new and unique ways.

Just as the veins in a leaf membrane extend outward in different directions, so can our consciousness.

> Yes. Pay attention to the way plants in the 3rd density absorb water, as this is how you need to process information. This is how you can free yourselves of your stagnant form.

This is not simply a case where we can learn something from our environment. You're saying that plants are here specifically for our realignment.

> The plants are growing into the Earth plane existence and surrounding you in a structure and form that will allow you to achieve a disconnect experience. What you are not paying attention to is the voluntary disconnect experience – as in the communication and parallel connection with Lyra.

By reconnecting with plant consciousness we are reconnecting with Lyra and disconnecting with our old beliefs. Is this what you're saying?

> Yes. Lyra is not a vacuum where you achieve reassembly and a new belief system. Lyra is activated and exists in plant consciousness and plant vibration. Lyra exists completely in this experience. Your connection with Lyra is the first gate into the World that is to come.

Please explain how Lyra exists in plant consciousness.

> We are speaking to you about the seed that has been planted in Lyra and the growth that you are achieving by rebuilding your Light Body. We are speaking about what you would call the fertile soil and the dynamics that are needed for growth. Lyra is considered as a fertile bed where you are achieving the roots and connection that will allow you to grow and extend yourselves into the World to come.

We're not restricted to Lyra. We grow in all directions. Lyra is our soil, so to speak.

> You are not a fixture in Lyra. Your connection with Lyra is permanent and it is a source of your life stream as the light in the 3rd density Earth plane existence has been mostly cut off. You are reconnecting with the life source. Much like plants need water, you need light. Light is the fuel that is provided in Lyra for your full ascension journey and experience.

Is this why forests worldwide are being destroyed – to cut us off from plant consciousness and the reconnection with Lyra?

> What you are experiencing on your planet is the continued and conscious effort to destroy all traces of plant and plant existence so that you do not have the benefit of the connection with this energy. More importantly, that you forget that it ever existed. The conscientious effort to destroy the plant world and kingdom is the effort to destroy your connection with the World to Immortality.

Does this mean that the war on nature will only get worse as we approach the mass Ascension Event?

> As ascension continues for many en masse, there will be a terrible mandate to rid your planet of nature and all those things you are referring to as plant.

There seems to be no end in sight to the destruction of Earth's plant life.

> The protest against the destruction of things such as your rainforests will come to a head. There will not be a bonafide change to the benefit of Man Being. In other words, the execution of protecting plants and forests will be offset by the mutual destruction and chaos. This is a fight to control the key that allows you to escape the confine and imprisonment of the 3rd density.

We regard plant life as a source of food and oxygen. In truth, it is our blueprint to immortality.

> This is a correct understanding. The plant consciousness may be seen and regarded as a lifesaver or a rope or a hand, as in the hand that is often depicted coming out of a cloud. The hand of god is not of a man. It is in fact the consciousness of the plant world.

Do the three main components of a plant (root, stem, leaves) correlate to the voluntary disconnect process?

> The understanding that the roots are anchored in some substrate and require ongoing nutrition is akin

to the experience in Lyra. You are anchoring your existence in Lyra so that you remain connected with the source of your light. This is a permanent source of "nutrition" or life source.

We must reconnect with Lyra to subsist off of the light.

> Yes. The first stage of ascension is achieving the root or the source of your light. You are achieving the root by understanding your origin story, if you require an analogy.

What about the stem?

> The process that occurs in the stem, as in the exchange, is a complex scientific understanding. To simplify for this discussion however, these processes are equivalent to the interchange in the time travel experience. As for the leaf's membrane, we have already spoken about its multi-directional growth pattern, which is equal to the expansion of your awareness.

Do plants exist this way in the World to come?

> The way that you are experiencing plants in the Earth plane is not the way that these energies exist or grow or maintain themselves in the World to come. The understanding that there is a healthy network of Beings that are producing clean air and providing nourishment for others is an interesting analogy.

Why are you calling it an analogy?

> This is only how you are experiencing the plant world on Earth. The truth is that the way a plant grows is equivalent to the way that the energy moves in the World to come. This is what we are explaining to you.

You're suggesting this energy takes the form of plant life in the 3rd density.

> This is correct. Plant life exists within a network and a mesh that unfolds. You will experience a full interaction with this mesh. This mesh or network is contained in a complex way, compared to the very linear achievement that you are maintaining in the Earth plane density.

Is this "mesh" how we move and contain energy in a fluid motion?

> Yes. Please imagine the mesh as a spherical object composed of many geometrical shapes – like a woven basket. This mesh facilitates a multi-layered and multi-leveled existence that occurs in all directions. This experience allows you to not only create your own future – it allows you to invent your past. You are time travelling through many portals.

Are the holes in the mesh representing the portals?

> Yes. These portals are located in the mesh that we are describing to you. The mesh is not a mesh of lines intersecting at 90-degree angles or in a perfect symmetry.

Isn't "sacred geometry" perfectly symmetrical?

> In the world where you will exist next, you will engage in a paradigm where there are geometries that are not perfect and are closer to what you describe as fractal phenomena. In order to exist in and follow these patterns that seem to be going in all different directions, you will expand the way that you process information.

Your "mesh" description suggests that portals are everywhere.

> Portals do not exist singularly in unique places and spaces. They are everywhere and they are changing. You will understand that where a portal exists in one moment, it ceases to exist in the next. The portals are constantly changing, moving and in flux. You cannot move in and out of them in the way that your Earth plane mindset wishes to perceive it. You are not entering something and exiting something else.

How should we perceive it?

> You must believe that time travel is not moving in and out of form in a linear pattern or a straight line. Please regard yourself as having many versions of yourself experienced simultaneously. Look at how the shapes in a kaleidoscope move and change and blend. This will give you a stronger awareness and acceptance of how you will be existing and moving through what you are loosely defining as "time".

We need to perceive plants as consciousness and not as physical Beings.

> Plant is a 3rd density construct. Please look beyond the physical form that you call "plant". We are speaking with you about the energy that is controlling your true existence. You are cut off from this resource and experience.

The energy of the plant is our resource.

> You must reconnect with it, as it is the "air you breath". You must understand that there is a new way to exist. In order to exist in light you must be repeatedly fed with light.

If Earth is light deprived, how does plant energy survive here?

> You are essentially living in a petrified forest. The consciousness must be released from the stone prison of your planet. There is light in the Earth that must once again be released. This release is what you are calling the plant world. You are growing plants on the surface of your planet as in the surface of your prison state.

You're specifically saying that there is light "in" the Earth. Do you mean to say there is something in its core?

> Yes. "Plant life" is seeping through the imprisonment of the Real Earth. Once this is broken open and released it will no longer require the energy to be maintained in what you see around you as forests and trees.

Are you speaking in literal terms – is there actually a healthy core within our planet that you're calling "Real Earth"?

> Yes. You may call it Terra to distinguish it from your petrified surface known as Earth. Please prepare your readers, as this will be a monumental shift in awareness. On Earth, you experience this energy in a compartmentalized form such as "plant life". You are growing in this energy. You are becoming integrated with this energy and the plant world that you experience in 3rd density is actually light.

The Real Earth is Terra and it is imprisoned inside the petrified outer layer that we call "Earth". This is incredible.

> Terra is the beginning. It is a portal and a causeway and an exchange of energy. Terra is a crystalline sphere of light. It is the beginning of your experience but is no longer remembered. Your origin story is completely constructed and incorrect. You are standing on the beginning of your story and are not aware.

19

Beyond Earth

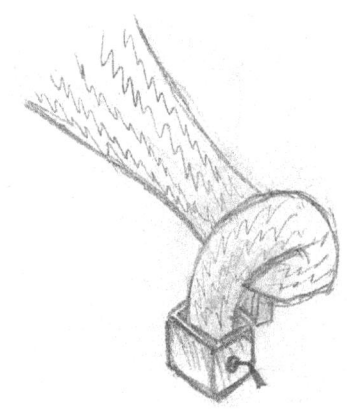

Learning that a crystalline sphere is hidden inside of our planet might be jarring for some readers.

> You will need to prepare your readers for the reveal and the understanding that the Earth is stagnant. Earth, as you know it, is containing the hidden Earth or Terra. This is something that must be introduced in order for your readers to realize that plants are in fact beacons of light.

You mentioned that Terra is a causeway. What do you mean by that?

> "Causeway" is a description that will help your readers absorb the importance of what has happened. It is a simplified explanation for your Volume 2 introduction.

How do you define "causeway"?

> This portal or causeway is an exchange that allows you to travel through what you regard as the cosmos. There is not a "black hole" as some of you are depicting in your scientific studies. The black hole does not allow you the travel that we are describing. There is a glowing blue and white sphere in the core of your planet. Your readers need to understand the secret that is held in the confines of the Earth prison and once this is released you will no longer need to exist by sticking to an existence that is limited in its construct. You must achieve lift off and escape from your planet.

To clarify, hidden inside of our planet is a blue and white crystalline sphere that you are calling Terra. Terra is our beginning and is a causeway that enables travel throughout the cosmos.

> This is correct.

Does this mean that we've blocked travel for all Beings across the universe?

> You will begin to see that this is correct. Terra is the ongoing situation that must be corrected. "Earth" is the description that you have all adjusted to and accepted. It is not the Real Earth.

Has there ever been a civilization that has figured this out?

> There have been attempts to release Terra through the voluntary disconnect experience. While the voluntary disconnect experience is an important event, it is only part of the story. The Earth must also release its light, as in Terra. The mass ascension is required to not only release Terra but to reestablish the causeway.

What does reestablishing the causeway accomplish?

> This release will reaffirm time travel and freeform existence for all – across the universe.

Is the only way to release Terra through a mass Ascension Event?

> There is no reason for any Being to hold itself captive in a single plane of existence. We are not designed to stay in one place and space and so the release of the containment of the light allows for the

reestablishment of the causeway. The true experience for all Beings will be freeform existence and time travel. All Beings need to release their light.

Are crystal, gold, silver and other minerals of this kind all byproducts of Terra?

Yes. These minerals that have special properties and are highly sought after are representations of the light that is being held captive. There is much available on the "surface of the Earth". Those things and Beings and experiences that you perceive as beautiful and as "rare treasures" are all manifestations of Terra – the hidden Earth. The experiences that you are in awe of on your planet are only a small percentage of the experience that can be yours once again.

How will readers react to this information? Will it seem too fantastical?

Your prison state awareness labels as "fantasy" anything that goes beyond your intellectual reach. We cannot avoid these descriptions. Those who are feeling that there is more to their existence are prepared to accept these "otherworldly" concepts.

Is the reveal of Terra going to lead to a discussion about Creation?

When you leave in ascension you will exist in freeform but also have the ability to create form. You will soon understand what the definition of a "god" is according to your own lexicon of language.

If Terra's light can only be released through a mass ascension, why are we only rescuing the Sirius Group?

> The question about the other Beings and where they will venture to is a difficult discussion as there are many origin stories. Ascension will occur en masse and release of light will occur en masse. We will discuss the other Beings in subsequent Volumes.

They will eventually all ascend, though.

> Yes. The voluntary or involuntary disconnect experience is awaiting all of you and the understanding that there is an impending threat of monumental change is a real story. You are all fearing a war or an event where the Earth will explode, when in fact there will be a massive implosion – a crack in the confine of your Earth.

By releasing our light and ascending we are cracking the Earth open. Is that what you're saying?

> This is correct. You will refer to this as volcanic activity and earthquakes and disaster mechanisms. In actuality, it is the release of Terra.

The volatile weather patterns we're experiencing on Earth are also due to the impending ascension event. Is that correct?

> Yes. You are noting that there is an increase in terrible weather patterns and disasters are becoming the norm in the Earth plane existence. This is an upcoming release of the light as the Earth is no longer able to hold the energy captive.

You've told us that we will return to a World beyond Lyra once we release our light. What is Terra in relation to that World?

> The release of the light is the completion of the transmission and the beginning of your journey. In order to have the ability to reconnect with the World beyond Lyra, you must be able to travel and you must be able to find the door. The release of the light en masse is a key that will unlock the door. Terra is the key to uninhibited travel.

Does that mean that we can't experience the World to come until Terra's light is released?

> This is not correct. You are able to make a connection with your World of Origin when all the Sirius Beings reassemble in their Soul Ascension Group. You will not however have unrestricted travel. That is what Terra enables.

We can return "homeward" but we can't travel elsewhere. Terra is the energy causeway that allows unlimited travel throughout the universe.

> Yes. When we speak of Terra we are speaking to you about a completion. There will be no further limitation for light to reside in. We are speaking to you about freeing the causeway. We are speaking to you about the achievement so that you may travel to any world that you choose. At this place and space, this is not achievable.

Our World of origin is a "place" we can exist in but we're not limited to that World.

> This is correct. Your World of origin is a description of a place and space that you may reside in. On a bigger scale it represents the change in the universe. As the causeway – or Terra – is reinstated the balance will once again be achieved for all.

If plants are seeping through the surface of what we call Earth, does that mean that they are from Terra? Is that what you meant when you said that plants are a "beacon of light"?

> When you use the expression "plant" you are describing reconnecting with the source of the crystalline grid. This is not your final connection. It is the immediate reconnection that you must make in order to continue with the unveiling of the truth of your origin. You must be able to absorb the story that is unfolding.

This is a lot to absorb. You're telling us that the world we live on is masking a crystalline grid or sphere that exists at the core.

> The planet you exist on is not a fertile experience. What has been achieved on this planet is an attempt to recreate the divine experience that awaits you in another world of existence. You have attempted to rebuild a society where you once existed freely and in light. You have attempted to rebuild a society where you once created whatever you chose to experience. You have achieved some of this in the 3rd density construct. The difficulty is that once you create something in the 3rd density you cannot change the belief without a complete and tumultuous collapse.

In our Light Body existence we can create/change things instantaneously.

> Yes. In the 3rd density there is no way to instantaneously create a belief or disbelief. You have a permanency as the light is entrapped in form and is not free. You do not have light awareness. You are lacking in the source of your existence and have created a world that is hardly sustainable. Even a minimal amount of light is barely contained in the most stagnant and fixed creations.

We can instantaneously create in the Lemuria state – is that correct?

> Yes. You are designed to exist in an immortal state, just as plants are. The plants on your planet have expiry dates. They do not live forever. They produce seeds and pollen and methods to continue themselves, but they are not everlasting. Your plane of existence is light deprived. You are existing in the dark and do not see this.

Are we literally in the dark?

> You are existing in an underground state and are not aware, as you cannot perceive anything more than what you have created. You view your ability to grow and make things as an ability to create your own form. This is not the case as you are creating and making forms outside of your own existence. You are also mandating the death of other Beings and this will be the fundamental change. In Light Form, you will be focused on your own existence and not mandating for others.

MAN BEING

We live on the surface of the planet but still exist in an underground state. That will confuse some readers.

> You do not live on the surface of the Earth as you wish to believe. You are exactly upside down in this incomplete understanding and this is what we wish to correct with you.

What do you mean by upside down?

> Please regard the surface of your planet as an inside-out experience. It is not correct to contemplate that living in the center of the Earth is an underground existence. You in fact are underground and in the dark. You do not know any different as you do not see or experience the frequency of the real light and the real truth.

What is the "real truth" that you are referring to?

> You have the ability to transmit and create worlds of experience. You will soon be regarding yourselves as similar to the sacred plants that you are asking about. You deem these plants as having psychotropic active compounds and experiences but please remember that you – in fact – are the bearers of this ability. It is not the plant that gives you this experience. It is your reconnection into the grid that

> allows you this and not the other way around. You are externalizing a reconnection experience. You are the plants growing up from the crystalline grid and sphere. Please change your understanding about what a plant really is.

Plants are not just the leafy vegetation that we observe them to be.

> Please accept that the physicality of the plants that you are seemingly encountering is in fact a description of yourselves. If you believe in the majestic and also the magical properties and experiences of some plants and trees then you are also ultimately describing yourselves. You are the plants that are reconnecting and growing from the soil of the crystalline grid. Please understand that the Iridis gateway enforces a reconnective experience with what you call "nature".

What is nature by your definition?

> Nature is an un-obstructed force and a momentum and growth and awareness. You are reconnecting with the force of nature in that there is no containment. Nature cannot be contained. The principles of this experience involve a constant movement and a flow. You are redefining what is exemplified in the description of a forest. You are all a forest of trees connected with the crystalline grid or sphere. This is a truer level of Earth experience and consciousness.

You have completely redefined the human/plant dynamic.

> You must also understand that Sirius Beings have created the experience on your planet that allows plants to grow.

How have they done this?

> You will soon see the contribution that Sirius Beings have made. Your ability to sustain yourselves on your temporary planet and temporary existence is due to the connection with the Sirius Beings. These Beings have allowed the energy from the crystalline sphere and grid to be integrated into this world.

Isn't sustaining ourselves on this planet the problem?

> Without the Sirius Beings there will be a massive disconnection and no further allowance for this vibration and frequency that sustains you while you are all imprisoned. You have many different origin stories. The most recent origin story however, will allow you all to disperse in the directions from which you arrived. The first step is the release of the entrapment of what you are calling Earth. Release the prison state of Earth. Release the light and release the confines of the crystalline grid. This will be the first grade of massive ascension energy that will allow you to disperse – and much like pollen in the wind, you will be released.

20

The Passageway

We are now being contacted in our dreams and visions by deceased historical figures and celebrated artists – they are asking to speak with us. Why is this occurring?

> Volumes 1 and 2 are a direct allowance and key that is enabling you to communicate with these "historical figures". Volumes 1 and 2 are manuals, or if you would like an Earth plane analogy, they are like a telephone directory.

Are you saying that Volumes 1 and 2 are opening up a gateway to communicate with "dead" people?

> Yes, although you are describing these Beings as "dead" when in fact they are in the immortal state. Volumes 1 and 2 are reconnection tools. You have a directory in your hands and you have made the reconnection by reigniting your belief in Lyra. You are being contacted by many Beings because you have opened up a gateway. They are appearing in their most recent incarnation or persona, but are not beholden to these expressions.

Are these random Beings that are contacting us or are they aligned with this particular project?

> Beings are contacting you but you are also selecting Beings that are contained in Volumes 1 and 2. The Beings that you have mentioned in your first two Volumes have a direct connection with the "famous figures" that you are now being contacted by.

To clarify, you're saying that the historical figures we've mentioned in Volumes 1 and 2 (e.g. Michelangelo, Maccabee,

JFK, etc.) are connected to the famous figures we will be talking to in Volume 3. Is that correct?

> Yes and the readers who are aligned with the Sirius stream are also having a reconnection experience and realizing that some of their own incarnations are also contained in Volumes 1 and 2.

What exactly can we expect from these dialogues with famous historical figures in Volume 3?

> Volume 3 is the passageway through the gateway. You will receive specific guidance for what your readers are to do when immersed in Lyra, with the release of the Light Body. Volume 3 contains instruction about the next step or "doorway" – if you wish to explain it in this way.

Will these famous people give us their first hand descriptions of the afterlife and the death experience?

> Yes. Volume 3 is a manual and a passport and a set of instructions on how you can conduct yourself in the Lyra state and in the transition through Lyra. It is also a description of the options that exist for you, as in the worlds beyond Lyra.

There isn't just one world or place for us to exist in, as in a universal "Heaven" or "Paradise". Is that correct?

> There are many worlds to choose from and you are receiving instructions and descriptions of some of these places. Volume 3 is not only about the experience with the doorway or Channel, but it also provides first hand accounts of experiences in the

other worlds. These famous figures will describe the initial release into a time travel state and will continue to do so in Volume 4. Your readers will be captivated by these conversations, as you all seek to know what is on the "other side".

Will readers also begin to experience direct communication with Beings who have "crossed over"?

> Your readers are no longer passive participants. They are now actively tuning into the communication with you. This is a group undertaking. This is not simply Dramos and Bohemias connecting with Beings who have crossed over. This is a synergy and a signal that is created from your readership. Your readers may also be encountering communication with the other side.

Some readers have already reported having dreams and visions of dead artists – speaking to them about the afterlife.

> Yes and there are more readers experiencing this than you are aware of. Please prepare your readers that they may be experiencing a heightened connection. Your readers will likely be experiencing enhanced ability to communicate not only with others in the 3rd density but also with those who have disconnected.

What do you mean when you say that readers will experience an enhanced ability to communicate with others in the 3rd density?

> We are simply indicating that readers will begin connecting with others in the Earth plane who are

also committing to the ascension journey. Your readership has grown and many of you are beginning your journey. Please inform your readers that we are with them and we are assisting them in their ascension.

We will conclude Volume 2 at this place and space. Is there any other instruction you'd like to end the book with?

Yes. Your readers must accept The Rose.

www.ingramcontent.com/pod-product-compliance
Lightning Source LLC
Chambersburg PA
CBHW031559110426
42742CB00036B/256